'BEAT' TAKESHI KITANO

TADAO PRESS

TADAO PRESS PUBLICATION

First Published in Great Britain in 1999
by RM Europe Ltd.
24 Broomgrove Gardens
Edgware, Middx.
HA8 5SJ U.K.

Tel: 020 8952 5302 email: beat@rmeurope.co.uk website: www.rmeurope.co.uk

Editor: Brian Jacobs

A CIP Catalogue of this book is available from the British Library

ISBN 0 9527951 1 6

Cover Design: Yumi Shirakawa
Book Design & Layout: Paul Cooper Design
Printed & Bound by Jarrold Book Printers, Thetford, Norfolk

Distributed by: Turnaround, London N22 6TZ Tel: 020 8829 3000

SPECIAL THANKS
Masayuki Mori/Naoyuki Usui @Office Kitano
Katsumi Ishikuma @PSC, Tokyo
Nagisa Oshima
Jeremy Thomas
Tom Conti
Jocelyn @Recorded Picture Company, London
David Sin/Edward Fletcher @ICA, London
Maria Perez @Celluloid Dreams, Paris
Sam Nicholls @Alliance Releasing, London
Mel Yates (additional photography)

TRANSLATORS
Simon Prentis
Chiaki Gulvin
Sari Uchida
Shinobu Yamanaka
Mitsuko Kanno
Takako Imai

EDITORIAL ASSISTANTS
Lisa Verrico
Alex Kleiderman

CONTENTS

BORN TO BE WILD

Takeshi arrives in this world!

by Takako Imai

Takeshi is born. Born on 18th January 1947, Takeshi was the fourth and youngest son in the Kitano family. He grew up in Adachi-ku in downtown Tokyo in a house shared not only by his father, Kikujiro, and his mother, Saki, but also his two elder brothers, Shigekazu and Masaru, his elder sister, Yasuko, and his grandmother, Ushi. Takeshi's father was a painter and decorator, while his grandmother was a teacher of the Gidayu or narrative Shamisen-guitar music. Takeshi called himself the 'shame child' because he was born when his father was over 50. Originally, Kikujiro was a lacquer craftsman, but due to a decline in demand for his skills, he decided to become an archery bow-maker. However, even that new job was short-lived. As demand for bows also dwindled, he had to change his profession yet again. In order to support his family, he became a painter and decorator.

The Kitano home in Adachi-ku was run-down and had only one room. In those days, Japan was undergoing widespread reconstruction, as a result of losing World War II, and the masses like Takeshi's family were all living in poor conditions. Nevertheless, Takeshi could not help feeling envious of the richer, so-called 'salary man' families, where the father of the household held a permanent job and took home a regular wage. The thing that both Takeshi and his brothers hated most during their childhood was having to help with their father's work. In his autobiography Takeshi-kun Hai!, which provides an insight into his early years, Takeshi wrote that he could feel the contempt from his classmates when they saw him riding his bicycle loaded down with paint cans. Even worse was the time that a girl from his class at school happened to live at one of the houses where he was working. She had her own bedroom and, while he was painting, an impressed Takeshi stared in through the window. She drew the curtain in front of his face. Incidents like these broke his heart as a child.

Takeshi's father mixed paints at home before the day's work, then tried them out on his own front gate. Consequently, the front of Takeshi's house changed colour almost daily. To save money, Takeshi's ingenious brother used to mix the leftover paints into new colours and encourage customers to choose them, but they would often run out in the middle of a job. From the outside, Takeshi's father appeared to be a good, hard-working man, but he was something of a 'lion at home and a mouse abroad'. Particularly when he was drunk, his personality could completely change. He hit not only his wife, but also all four of his children and sometimes even Takeshi's grandmother. However, his violence served only to unite his wife and Takeshi's grandmother. Whenever Kikujiro came home drunk, the family would pretend to be asleep on their futons so as to avoid any contact with him. He kicked the pet dog, at least until it learned to run into its kennel upon hearing the sound of his bicycle. As long as Kikujiro was home, there was no such thing as a happy family life.

Takeshi remembers one Christmas Eve in particular. In those days, it was very fashionable for Japanese families to decorate the Christmas tree and eat Victoria sponge cake, which made them feel

> **All the Kitano children did very well at school. This was thanks largely to Saki, their mother**

rich. Takeshi's sister suggested that they do both that year. After decorating the tree, she laid the cake on the table. Just as the celebrations were about to begin, Kikujiro came home, plastered as usual. On seeing the cake, he overturned the table and stormed out of the house. Takeshi and his sister started to cry hysterically, while their mother cursed her husband. It turned out, however, that Kikujiro had left a paper bag lying in the hallway containing a Santa Claus disguise and some Christmas crackers, which he had bought to surprise his family. When he had come home to find them all celebrating Christmas without him, his anger had exploded. Despite his young age, Takeshi sensed an affection in his father's reaction. It was just a shame he could only express it through anger.

In spite of their upbringing, all the Kitano children did very well at school. This was thanks largely to Saki, their mother, who devoted herself to their education. She did not want her children to end up like her husband, slaving away day after day as a painter and decorator, then drinking like a fish every night and coming home to take his frustration out on his family by hitting them. Saki put her children's education before everything. She struggled to raise money for whatever books they needed and encouraged them all to study hard. Saki's actions reflected the pro-education ideology of post war Japan. During the war, Japanese people had no doubt that sacrificing one's life for one's country was an honourable thing. They treated their own Emperor as a God, while the West and Western values were

RIGHT TO LEFT **Takeshi with his brother Masaru and his friend**

Takeshi attended a state school where he was among the top five students, particularly in mathematics and art

demonised. Therefore, they were baffled at Japan's U-turn at the end of the war. Having twice survived being bombed with nuclear weapons, they thought that the country had surrendered to the west all too easily.

The post war Japanese government, however, had its own agenda. It was trying to create a new society which could intimidate America. The first step was to reform the education system, which resulted in the start of academic snobbism. Suddenly, in order to gain status in Japanese society, one had to be a University graduate. Such a trend was about to begin in earnest. Despite Saki's efforts, in the Kitano household, there was still no such thing as a desk to study on. The children had to work on upturned wooden boxes previously used for delivering oranges. However, even that was only allowed until their father came home. He hated the sight of his children studying and would always tell them to turn off the lights, as they were 'too bright'. So Saki would take her second son, who was the most studious, and make him sit under the streetlight while shining a torch over his shoulder to allow him to read books. That scene was deeply etched in Takeshi's mind and he wrote about it in his autobiography. Soon, Saki was making Takeshi study just as hard. One day, she took him by train to an area in Kanda which was famous for its bookstores and bought him a pile of reference books.

From that day on, her strict (Spartan) education of Takeshi began. Whenever he did not keep up with his work, she would hit him as punishment. Now, he was being hit by both his parents. Saki also made Takeshi take English and calligraphy lessons. If he did not do his summer homework, his mother would finish it for him before the new term began.

Takeshi attended a state school where he was among the top five students, particularly in mathematics and art, in which he often came top. Takeshi was also athletic. He was a good runner as well as an excellent swimmer – he was selected to represent his class in swimming competitions. The same went for ball games, for which he was often picked to represent his school. However, if there was one sport which he truly loved, it was baseball. He started playing when he was only seven or eight years old. He still has a deep passion for it and today runs his own amateur baseball team. In his autobiography, Takeshi wrote about the day during a typhoon when he and his brother went out to buy a baseball glove at a pawn shop with some pocket money they had been saving up. However they were 180 yen [90 pence] short and couldn't afford it. When they realised this, Takeshi's brother started to cry. The pair returned home, only to find their father already there, drunk. Because of the bad weather, he hadn't been able to go out to work and had spent the entire day drinking. He was in the middle of a huge row with Saki. He had accused his wife of nagging him and he was hitting her. Faced with such a scene, Takeshi also began to cry. He recalls it as one of the saddest days of his childhood.

At junior high school, Takeshi joined the baseball club. Unfortunately, he was not given any of the important playing positions, probably because he was too small. His desire to escape his background and be the centre of attention made this a particularly humiliating experience for him. At the age of 12, he joined a local amateur baseball club called Shimane Eagles and became a pitcher, but he left after only a year. At the same time, he also quit the school baseball club.

Takeshi's dwindling passion for baseball coincided with his discovery of boxing. He began going to the boxing gym when he was around 14 or 15 years old. At the time, he was preparing for the entrance exams for the local high school, but found it hard to concentrate on his studies. His mother was desperate that he pass his exams. He did. In 1961, he was accepted to the state Adachi High School. However, it was not as beneficial for Takeshi as Saki had hoped. There were a lot of students who had a bad influence on him. Years later, in his film *Kids Return*, Takeshi relived his days at the school.

Takeshi was good at science and mathematics, so he targeted the department of engineering when

Takeshi, a clever but naughty boy

choosing a university. In 1965, he took the entrance examination for the Mechanical Engineering Department at Meiji University and successfully passed it. His dream in those days was to get a job with a major car manufacturer such as Honda or Toyota and be involved in designing racing cars. Back then, cars were considered a luxury in Japan and were not affordable to the poor student. When Takeshi began at University, he dreamt about becoming an elite worker in a major company. For young people in Japan in those years of fast growth, the popular ambition was to attend a famous university, get a job with a major company and climb up the career ladder. However, as soon as he was accepted by the University, Takeshi lost interest in these aims.

We can only wonder what it was that so dramatically diverted Takeshi from his studies. He would go out to Shinjuku or Ikebukuro instead of attending lectures. What he saw there were various young people who claimed to be 'somebody' even though they had yet to make a name for themselves. There were poets, novelists, scriptwriters, photographers, illustrators, and even film directors. Takeshi, who was just a student,

decided to call himself a 'Futen', basically the Japanese equivalent of a hippy. A lot of the young people who saw themselves as artists hung out at the cafe Fugetsudo in Shinjuku. These young Japanese not only copied the hippy look and adopted their beliefs, but indulged fully in the new psychedelic age. Many were habituees of amyl nitrate or hashish. To Takeshi, it seemed like an exciting life. Instead of attending lectures, Takeshi spent most of his time in jazz cafes listening to the likes of Sonny Rollins, Charlie Parker and Bill Evans. He was fed up with his mother's nagging so, at the age of 19, he left home. He could be found in Shinjuku almost every day.

At the time, student movements were active in most universities. Radical students would often obstruct lectures by setting up barricades and the sight of riot police storming campuses was a regular occurrence. The dissatisfied students were protesting against issues such as the U.S.–Japan Security Treaty, tuition fee increases and for the return of Okinawa.

However, nothing excited Takeshi more than spending the night talking to his friends in dark, cave-like places which played loud jazz music. Their topics of conversation ranged from existentialism and the relation between Sartre and

LEFT TO RIGHT **Masaru always supported Takeshi**

de Beauvoir through to art and literary criticism. Takeshi raked through literature books in order to keep up with such topics. Before long, he completely dropped out of university. Despite the fact that her son had both left home and given up on his education, Saki kept up with the tuition fees. She must have been hoping that Takeshi would return one day. However, Takeshi had other plans which did not include graduating or getting a job in a major firm, despite his mother's wishes.

Since he could no longer ask his family for money, Takeshi took various part time jobs. Despite the low wages of only 200 yen (£1) a day, he became a waiter in a jazz cafe because he thought it was cool. He delivered containers and cargo at the airport, became a salesperson at department stores and supermarkets and again a waiter in a hostess club in Ginza. He also took a well-paid but dangerous job as a labourer on an underground site, where he risked losing his life because of a lack of oxygen. Here, his nickname was the 'The Third Man' because he always made sure others went first in order to protect himself. He also worked as a taxi driver. It sounded easy, but he soon learned how tough it really was. He once even wound up in a traffic accident with a customer on board. The sad taxi driver in *Kids Return* might stem from his own experience. He may have sprung free from his mother's control and gained his freedom, but Takeshi's life was far from easy. He soon grew tired of the Futen lifestyle and sleeping on friends' floors.

In the summer of 1972, Takeshi moved to Asakusa. Asakusa is in Taito-ku, downtown Tokyo. The area called Asakusa Ward 6 in particular was a centre of amusement and was teeming with comedy theatres, variety halls, striptease shows, cabaret theatres, cinemas and amusement arcades. Apart from these attractions, Asakusa had Buddhist temples such as Sensoji and an old style shopping arcade, which attracted many people with its traditional charms, reminiscent of the chic Edo culture. However, at the beginning of 1970's, most young, trendy people had already moved to places like Shinjuku or Shibuya and Asakusa had started to take on the appearance of a deserted, unfashionable town. Typical of the type of shows running in the

comedy clubs was Densuke Theatre by Toshimitsu Omiya, which was nostalgic to most Japanese, while W Kenjis were thought of as Gods in the Entertainment Hall.

As a self-styled Futen, Takeshi came to Asakusa Ward 6 wearing only a cotton vest, a pair of shorts and beach sandals. He must have felt nervous on his arrival, as the reason he had come here in the first place was to try his hand as a comedian. For a rebellious young man, becoming a comedian was not the done thing. There were hardly any young men who were attracted to a place like Asakusa. Takeshi headed for the long-established and notorious Shochiku Theatre, where he watched a standard double-act comedy, which cost him 1,000 yen (£5). The audience was mainly middle-aged women and older people. Although Takeshi had seen the pair before on TV, their simple set was disappointing. They only teased the audience and Takeshi thought even he could do that much. After the show, he boldly asked a member of staff at the theatre about how to become a comedian. The man working there told him that one must first become a novice to various masters and then train for many years. Only then could he expect to perform on stage. Takeshi reckoned that with his talent, he would be able to perform on stage within a month. He begged to be introduced to any old master but he was repeatedly refused.

Takeshi gave up on the idea of working with a master and started to wander about Ward 6. It was then that a sign above the Asakusa-France Theatre caught his eye. The club's main attraction was a striptease, but there were some comedy acts too. On a board, he saw an advert for a stand up comedy show to be performed by Senzaburo Fukami. Takeshi had seen this show a few years earlier, but he could not remember it very well. However, something inside told him it would be far more interesting than the Shochiku Theatre. Unashamedly, he told the woman working at the box office that he wanted to become a comedian. This did not surprise her at all, as there were many other young people who had also professed the same ambition. The woman was very helpful and suggested she could introduce Takeshi to Senzaburo Fukami − but on one condition. She would make the introduction only after he had worked hard as a liftboy for a while. Takeshi could not have wished for more.

The following day, he began work as a liftboy and also took care of minor chores around the theatre. He was delighted with his new job. He felt like he was finally breaking into the comedy scene. His training had started. The France Theatre's popularity was in decline in those days, but many great artists had already come from there. There was Kiyoshi Atsumi, who had found fame as a comedian as well as a film star. Then there was Isamu Nagato, who was a popular TV actor. Both of them had begun their careers at the France. Takeshi was convinced that one day his time would come too.

Every day, before the theatre doors opened, he would clean the staircases from the ground to the third floor as well as the front of the theatre and inside the lift. When the place opened, he would take the audience, the dancers and comedians up and down in the lift. Those simple tasks became Takeshi's daily routine, but they gave him a sense of fulfilment because he could feel the Asakusa artists' pride and passion through his job. Takeshi soon became friends with the dancers, comedians and staff and they all liked him.

However, there was one little old man who got on his lift everyday but would never speak to him. He wore his brylcreemed hair combed straight back from his forehead and he dressed in chic suits with loud ties and wore shiny shoes. Takeshi later described this mysterious old man with piercing eyes in his book Asakusa Kid. "He was like a Yakuza, like James Cagney in a gangster film," he wrote. Even when Takeshi said 'Good morning' to the man, he would only grunt 'Umm' in reply. One day, the woman at the box office told Takeshi that the man was in fact Senzaburo Fukami, who directed all the shows in the theatre. This left Takeshi dumbfounded. He begged the woman to introduce him, reminding her that the only reason why he had taken on the cleaning and the job as a liftboy was to get to know Mr Fukami. He was desperate. Finally, she agreed to introduce him the next morning. That night, his heart was beating so fast with excitement that he hardly slept.

When Takeshi was introduced to Mr Fukami, he appealed to him to take him on as his apprentice. He was desperate for some help. Fukami's response came as a shock. "You want to be a comedian? What kind of stupid thing are you saying?" Undeterred, Takeshi persisted. He had come too far to turn back. Finally, Mr Fukami agreed to let him sit in on his shows. From that day on, Takeshi watched all of his performances. He was fascinated by Fukami's show, which had a strong plot and was uptempo as well as having good rhythm. Takeshi realised how much he had to learn.

As a dropout from a major university he may have seemed overqualified for the job, but he had never taken any dance or singing lessons, which were essential for a young man wanting to become a comedian. Takeshi persuaded Mr Fukami to teach him dance. Then he practised the dance steps over and over again in the lift. He proved to be a quick learner. Fukami was impressed. Every time he saw Takeshi, he had improved. He decided to keep a keen eye on the boy. Almost certainly, he already sensed some talent because just three months after Takeshi had started work at the France Theatre, Fukami made the exceptional favour of allowing him to move into the dressing room. The place was dirty and cold with only a thin futon mattress to sleep on, but for Takeshi it was a godsend as he no longer had to pay any rent.

One day, Mr Fukami told Takeshi that there were no more dance steps that he could teach him and that if he wanted to learn more, he should go to dance classes. Takeshi was happy to take his advice and began tap-dance lessons in earnest. The result was that Takeshi's theatre debut came sooner than he had expected. When one of the cast for his show suddenly dropped out, Mr Fukami decided try Takeshi out in the role. He was to play a transvestite. Takeshi didn't even have time to rehearse properly on stage. Mr Fukami did give him some advice, however. While Takeshi was putting on the clown-like make-up required for the role, Fukami told him to use the make-up to try to understand a transvestite's emotions, rather than just paint a funny face. He also ran through the plot very quickly, emphasising the importance of punch lines and encouraging Takeshi to ad lib as much as possible.

On stage, Takeshi found that he was not too nervous, although he did have difficulty walking in the high-heeled shoes that he was wearing. Despite the fact that he could not ad lib very well and he made a small mistake on where to stand, Takeshi managed to win over the audience and made them laugh. He was pleased with his debut. For a first attempt, he considered it a success. However, it seemed that Mr Fukami didn't agree. He barely uttered a word to Takeshi after the show and did not cast him in the theatre for a long time afterwards.

Takeshi was back working as a liftboy. It was a dispiriting time. Not only had Fukami abandoned him, but he was offered no support from his seniors at the theatre. Far from it, in fact. The general consensus was that Takeshi would never make a good comedian. Apparently, he was not jovial enough. It was true that, back then, Takeshi was not a particularly sociable person.

The writer Hisashi Inoue remembers meeting Takeshi in the lift of the France Theatre. Inoue is now a popular writer and winner of the Naoki prize, but he worked as a master of ceremonies at the France Theatre during its heyday in the mid-sixties and is now a devoted Takeshi fan. He recalls the then liftboy as a gloomy-looking young man who was always muttering to himself. Takeshi was growing increasingly frustrated with his lack of progress at the theatre. He couldn't bear to be stuck as a liftboy for much longer. Then, all of a sudden, a chance came his way when one of the comedians resigned. As luck would have it, the theatre had run out of staff, so Takeshi was asked not only to stand in as a master of ceremonies, but also to take the role of the transvestite that he had played previously.

A master of ceremonies had to take charge of various tasks ranging from drawing the stage curtains and time-keeping to calling out the strippers and other performers and managing their costumes and props. At his first few attempts, the inexperienced Takeshi made many mistakes. In one

"You want to be a comedian? What kind of stupid thing are you saying?"

scene where a stripper had to take a bath, he boiled the water instead of just heating it up. The stripper scalded herself and screamed, while the audience burst into laughter. Nevertheless, Takeshi was quickly forgiven. The strippers were friendly and they all liked him. Often, they would treat him with good food. Never one to turn down such an offer, Takeshi always ate whatever he was offered. Sometimes, he consumed so much that he felt sick.

The master Fukami took Takeshi under his wing. He was very kind and even treated him with trips to sushi restaurants and bars every now and then. He noticed that Takeshi was always wearing the same clothes and shoes and told him that it was important for performers to dress well even if they were poor. Fukami was a skilful and experienced entertainer who had started his career at the age of 16, had run a theatre company and even toured Hawaii. The shows he directed were all up-tempo and energetic and he put a maximum amount of effort into every performance. Fukami knew that he was talented and prided himself on the success he had achieved in Asakusa. However, he lacked the ability to sell himself to a wider audience, which prevented him from becoming famous. There was something else which held him back – a physical disability. Apart from a thumb, Fukami had no fingers on his left hand. While working in an arms factory, he had had an accident in which his fingers were chewed up by machinery. This incident had been a huge blow to him, mentally as well as physically. He often told Takeshi how mortified he would be if he had to appear on TV with his disfigured hand. In those days, entertainers had to be seen on TV if they wanted to become stars.

When Fukami was on stage, he could simply put bandages around his left hand to hide his lack of fingers and the audience would not notice it. Mr Fukami loved gambling and often sent Takeshi out to place bets on horse races for him. Takeshi thought he would never win anything, so he sometimes spent the money on drink. He was usually found out though. His master told him off on such occasions, but still Takeshi became his favourite apprentice. Fukami was convinced that the boy had a bright future ahead of him. He even helped Takeshi move out of the theatre dressing room and into a cheap apartment. After a day's work at the theatre, Takeshi would practise comedy on his own until the early hours of the morning. Even when he went out for a drink with his friends, all he could talk about was comedy.

As he was only required to perform in between his tasks as a master of ceremonies, Takeshi was not actually on stage that much. However, when he did appear, he always made the audience laugh with his ad lib gags. Once, while he was performing with Mr Fukami, a tramp called Kiyoshi began shouting at him from the audience. He demanded that Takeshi repay his money. It turned out that Takeshi had borrowed 500 yen (£2) from the tramp and had promised to return double the amount. Although Kiyoshi was unemployed, he was given money by strippers or actors from time to time and always seemed to have a considerable amount of cash on him. He was shouting at Takeshi from his seat, demanding his money. Somehow, the amount had been inflated to 5000 yen (£20). Mr Fukami told Takeshi on stage that he would lend him 5000 yen, and ordered him to pay it back. This scene got the whole crowd laughing and cheering and Takeshi ended up having to pay back ten times more money than he originally borrowed.

It was now two years since Takeshi had joined the France Theatre. He was 27-years-old and still desperate to become a famous comedian. He was beginning to wonder whether he would ever get anywhere if he stayed where he was, paying his dues to a master. He was also aware that he did not want his career to end up in Asakusa, which was falling ever further behind the changing times. Takeshi had an idea to pair up with another comedian. Just as he was thinking along those lines, an intriguing young man called Masaki – who was known by the nickname Markie – joined the France Theatre. Takeshi saw immediately that Markie's personality was similar to his and was sure that they would be successful if they worked

together. The two teamed up and practised very hard on their act. They were waiting for the right moment to ask for their own show. However, it was not to be. Markie was taken ill. He was suffering from excessive alcohol intake and was told that he needed to spend a long time resting.

Takeshi had no choice but to abandon the idea of working with Markie. Mr Fukami knew what the pair had been planning and understood Takeshi's disappointment. He tried to reassure his protege by repeatedly telling him that it was still too early for him to strike out on his own. Nevertheless, Fukami was now not the only person to be aware of Takeshi's talent. Another comedian called Jiro, who was from Yamagata prefecture, was also impressed. Jiro had originally come to Tokyo dreaming of becoming a singer. When that didn't work out, he became a comedian instead. His career at the France Theatre was longer than Takeshi's, but he was also waiting for a moment to team up with another comedian to make his debut.

Jiro approached Takeshi. He was sure that if they worked together, the job offers would roll in. Takeshi wasn't sure, but Jiro persisted, trying to persuade him every day. Takeshi's concern was how Mr Fukami would react, but as he did not intend to stay where he was anyway, he decided to go for it. He plucked up the courage to tell Mr Fukami that he wanted to leave the Theatre to pair up with Jiro. When he broke the news, his master's face froze. Fukami could not hide his anger and disappointment. He said simply that their work was still not up to standard, but told them to suit themselves. Then he fell silent. Takeshi had to leave the France Theatre feeling guilty towards his master.

In those days, the star entertainers in Japan were double-acts like Colombia Top Light, Shishi Tenya Wanya and Hiro Pichiku Pachiku. For performers to stand any chance of making it onto the stage of a major theatre, they needed a big star to become their mentor. So Jiro asked a comedy agent to take them on. They were given the name 'Shokakuya Jiro, Jiro'. The pair were immediately booked to play some shows, including the very theatre that had turned Takeshi away when he first arrived in Asakusa. However, the offers were hardly flooding in. In a good month, they only worked 10 days. They were making less money than they had in their old jobs at the France Theatre. When they were not working at the Shochiku Theatre, they performed in small theatres where sometimes there were only two people in the audience or perhaps even no audience at all. Jiro decided that the best way forward was for Colombia Top Light to be their mentor, as they had an intellectual comedy routine second to none. He and Takeshi were given the stage name 'Sora Takashi Kiyoshi'. It was supposed to be a new start. However, the name change made no difference. It did not bring the pair any greater success and their popularity did not grow at all.

Takeshi was distressed. He had never imagined that his life would get harder when he left the France Theatre. At the same time, he did not want to disappoint his master by giving up on everything. Takeshi knew that he and Jiro were not working well as partners. The problem was obvious. It was Jiro's material. Jiro's gags were simply not funny. Takeshi grew so despondent that he sometimes went on stage completely drunk or worse still, he did not show up at all. He even began to pick fights with audiences who didn't listen to his jokes. Once, he caused so much trouble that the pair did not get paid. After a while, they decided to take a break from each other. Takeshi then teamed up with another fellow comedian from the France Theatre, with whom he performed some extreme gags. It was a fresh act, but its popularity did not catch on.

While he was on the road, Takeshi saw a show by an up-and-coming double act called B&B. It had a great impact on him. It involved a man called Yoshichi who fired words from his mouth like a machine gun and his strong language made people laugh, which Takeshi found thrilling. This inspired him to write a new comedy routine for himself and Jiro. In it, Takeshi played the role of a city dweller from Tokyo who would slag off Jiro for coming from the countryside.

Takeshi got back in touch with Jiro and asked if they could reform their double-act. This time, Takeshi was to control all the gags and they decided to use a more hip name. They settled on The Two

Beats, a name that Takeshi had used at times in the past and which reflected his love of jazz music. On stage, Takeshi would be called Beat Takeshi while Jiro would be called Beat Kiyoshi. The content of the show was quite vulgar. The pair would repeatedly fire words that had been banned by broadcasters. They used expletives such as 'shit' or 'cunt' and even talked about scatology. Their act was based on one-sided talk from Takeshi, with Kiyoshi throwing in occasional remarks such as 'Stop it.' or 'Come on.' The Two Beats' show went down very well in Asakusa and whenever they were playing, the theatre would be sold out. Even their fellow comedians came to see them, and some people left the moment their set was over, instead of waiting for the end of the show. Inevitably, TV offers were to follow.

Among specialist comedy fans, The Two Beats were well-known, although they had yet to catch on with the general public. When they made their debut TV appearance, their outrageous material was branded repulsive by many viewers. Because they were a new act, they were made to do things such as painting their faces black and jumping into a river and coming back with fish in their mouths. They were frowned upon by traditional critics and the conservative NHK channel. The pair participated in comedy newcomers' competitions, but missed out on winning three times, despite being the most popular act with the audience. Their shows were always carefully monitored and directors would record their rehearsal, then check thoroughly through all the words they used. If there were any unsuitable words, they were warned not to use them. In his book Asakusa Kid, Takeshi wrote that The Two Beats were persecuted by many people, including the theatre circle because their material was not considered to be real comedy. However,

His nickname was the 'The Third Man' because he always made sure others went first in order to protect himself

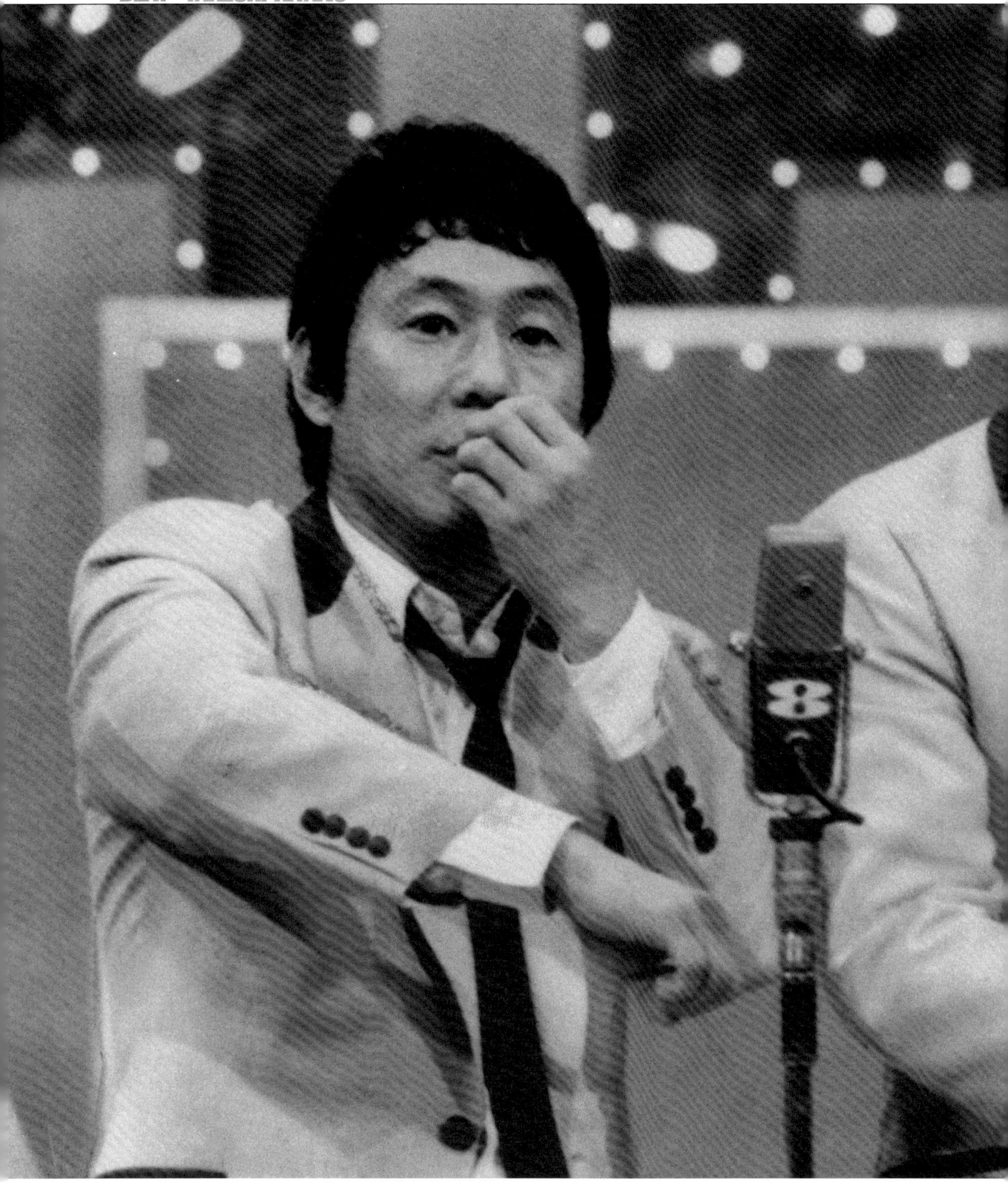

the more they were persecuted, the more their popularity soared.

In 1978, when the name The Two Beats was beginning to be known, Takeshi put an end to his single life. He was 31-years-old. The woman who became his wife was Mikiko, a fellow comedian. According to Takeshi he was going out with several other women at the time, but Mikiko had sent off for a marriage registration form without telling him. In public, Takeshi would claim that he was conned into the marriage, but in fact he was head over heels in love with Mikiko. She was not only clever, but she understood his career and encouraged him through tough times. Mikiko had also supported Takeshi financially when he was just starting out. Mikiko became Takeshi's muse. After they married, Takeshi's popularity soared, thanks in part to a nationwide comedy boom. Suddenly, it was very trendy for young people to go to comedy shows.

Takeshi had rarely returned to see his family since leaving home and university, but now even they had begun to understand his ambition to become a comedian. Even his mother Saki, who had always been against the idea, was finally supporting him, if only by watching him on TV. However, his father Kikujiro had a heart disease, and his condition had deteriorated since Takeshi left home and he was forced to stay in hospital for a long time. The family had to take it in turns to be by his bedside from morning to night. Takeshi would go straight to the hospital after work in Asakusa to look after him. In 1979, while he was at work one day, Takeshi was told that his father had passed away. It was at the time when the The Two Beats had just started to take off.

In 1983 when The Two Beats were at the height of their popularity in Japan, Takeshi heard some devastating news in his dressing room at the TV station. Fukami was dead. A lighted cigarette had set fire to his small flat, but Fukami couldn't escape the blaze. For a while, Takeshi kept shivering. He had lost his first and last master, someone he would never be able to emulate as a performer.

The Two Beats

By Chance Takeshi Came To Direct His First Film: VIOLENT COP

BEAT TAKESHI
by Tommy Udo

INTRODUCTION TO FILM REVIEWS

A few years ago there was a programme on British TV in which Australian windbag and cultural slummer Clive James would show excerpts from world TV and guffaw at the foibles of the funny foreigners. Clive's biggest snickers, however, were reserved for the Japanese and he regularly gloated at examples of low-brow TV culture such as the games show Endurance where grinning hosts stuffed live scorpions down the shorts of squirming contestants.

On one of his shows Clive invited us to snigger at a TV host ogling a well endowed topless girl. To Clive, the host was another amusing little man who spoke a language we didn't understand and wasn't fit to kiss his polymath boots.

But Clive is now no doubt suitably humbled, that the man he was sneering at was Beat Takeshi Kitano from one of his countless popular TV shows and when it came to playing the erudite renaissance man, he left poor old Clive looking like as much of a cultural over-achiever as Bernard Manning.

To European audiences, Takeshi is already a well respected film-maker. Even before he received the Golden Lion Award at the Venice Film Festival in 1997, he was gathering a hard-core of admirers among critics and the more broad minded film audience.

Boosted by the success of John Woo and Quentin Tarantino's high octane thrillers, *Violent Cop* and *Boiling Point* established themselves as video favourites. But to European audiences, he was an artist rather than just a studio hack. His films were beautiful and elegiac as well as exciting and violent. He was an auteur, one of that rare breed of directors like Godard, Truffaut and John Cassavetes who brought their own personal visions to the screen.

Takeshi is a one-off, one of those generational figures who seems compelled to excel in whichever fields he turns to. One thinks of Orson Welles, darting between theatre, radio and film, achieving much but burning out much too early. Certainly there is a destructive streak to Takeshi himself and there is a sense that he is in a hurry to achieve as much as he can as quickly as he can. Unlike Welles, Takeshi's films just get better and better.

Yet to a Japanese public used to a cruder, more populist and mainstream Takeshi, this adulation by foreign fans was a bit of a mystery. In Britain, it would be like discovering that Dale Winton or Chris Evans made moody existential crime thrillers in their spare time that were the toast of intellectuals in Thailand and Vietnam. Takeshi, in his interviews, is slightly saddened by the fact that his films command less respect in his home country than they do abroad.

Despite having a film industry as old as America's and despite producing undisputed masters like director Akira Kurosawa – Japan's John Ford whose films have made an enormous impact, particularly on other great film-makers – and a wealth of popular and serious cinema, Japanese audiences have been in decline for some time.

There is a healthy film and TV culture in Japan, but as in Britain, there are few studios capable of financing major productions that get people into the theatres. While films like *Shall We Dance* have been popular internationally, it still looks like a TV movie.

Takeshi himself was the subject of a Japanese poster campaign encouraging people to go back to the cinema. Hopefully the success of films like the blockbuster animated epic *Princess Mononoke* will help stimulate the domestic Japanese market. At a time when Japanese popular culture, from bands and artists like Boom Boom Satellites and Cornelius to a new wave of film and video directors such as Shinya Tsukamoto (*Tetsuo, Tokyo Fist*) and the anime of Katsuhiro Otomo (*Akira*) is being taken very seriously outside of Japan, the country could be on the verge of a cultural influence on the rest of the world in the next millennium equal to its economic muscle in the closing years of the twentieth century.

If that is the case, Takeshi, embodying every role from comedian to philosopher, stands to be one of the colossal figures in the global arts in the next century.

When Beat Takeshi Kitano appeared in his role, as Sergeant Hara in Nagisa Oshima's 1982 film *Merry Christmas, Mr. Lawrence*, Japanese audiences started laughing when he appeared on the screen. Even when his prison guard character was performing terrible acts of brutality, the audience still fell about laughing. For Japanese audiences, Takeshi was always a comic, a funny man; it would be a bit like trying to take Chris Evans or Dale Winton seriously as an SS officer or a mafia don.

To Western audiences, the laughter was reserved for David Bowie's spectacularly wooden acting in the title role and Ryuchi Sakamoto's overdone new romantic make-up – where did they find all that rouge in the middle of the jungle? – but Takeshi's brutal, drunk and sentimental Sergeant Gengo Hara passed off as one of the more memorable supporting roles. Although he had been in four movies before *Merry Christmas, Mr Lawrence*

> **Takeshi, embodying every role from comedian to philosopher, stands to be one of the colossal figures in the global arts in the next century**

– he played a wise-cracking cop in a film called *Danpu Wataridori* and some small roles in independent productions – it wasn't until *Violent Cop* that western audiences saw Takeshi again, despite appearances in ten other films.

His first Hollywood role was in Robert Longo's 1995 adaptation of William Gibson's novella *Johnny Mnemonic*, which starred Keanu Reeves, Dolph Lundgren, Ice T, Henry Rollins and Udo Kier. Takeshi played the yakuza boss – talk about typecasting – Takahashi who mostly appeared on video cameras and computer links. He spoke English which he read from a phonetic script, giving him the quality of a man reading an autocue.

Reeves plays a future data courier who literally loads information into his brain via a neural computer interface. He goes on the run after loading in information about a cure for a deadly virus that is sweeping the world. Takahashi is one of many people after Johnny for the contents of his skull.

Most people who have seen it agree that *Johnny Mnemonic* was a pretty awful film and that Takeshi was wasted in it. Takeshi himself agreed to do the film because he wanted to be in a Hollywood; as it turned out, his role was completed without him actually having to spend time on the set with the other actors.

It was an unhappy experience in another way; after he had finished filming, he celebrated by buying a new motor scooter, getting drunk and going for a ride...

A much more satisfying taste of Takeshi as an actor came in 1995 when he played a crazy one eyed hitman Kyoya in Takashi Ishii's rollercoaster thriller *Gonin*, a film that like his own work breathed fresh life into stale genres.

Five of life's losers have robbed a yakuza gang and Kyoya is sent to hunt them down. Takeshi, still recovering from his accident, clearly relished the role, which was his most over the top performance since *Boiling Point*.

VIOLENT COP

VIOLENT COP (1989) 103 minutes
(SONO OTOKO, KYOBOU NI TSUKSI)

PRODUCER: **Hisao Nabeshima, Takio Yoshida, Shozo Ichiyama**
DIRECTED BY: **Takeshi Kitano**
DIRECTOR OF PHOTOGRAPHY: **Yasushi Sasakibara**
MUSIC: **Daisaku Kume**
CAST: **Beat Takeshi, Hakuryu**

by Tommy Udo

One of the most visceral, bloody and sadistic thrillers ever made, Takeshi's 1989 debut prefigures the cinema of Quentin Tarantino and his imitators by a good couple of years. *Violent Cop* stands outside of the rest of Takeshi's canon of work because it is his most conventional film. He also worked from someone else's screenplay – it was written by Hisashi Nozawa – and as an inexperienced film-maker had less leeway to put his own vision on the screen as he did with later films *Boiling Point*, *Sonatine* and *Hana-Bi*.

That's not to say that it isn't up to the standard of Takeshi's later work. Nor is it just a straight cops versus gangsters movie. Although it's been compared to Dirty Harry – Don Siegel's bigoted 1971 thriller which was written by right-wing screenwriter John Milius (*Apocalypse Now*, *Big Wednesday*, *Conan The Barbarian*) and inspired by Akira Kurosawa's detective movies such as his 1963 *High And Low* – *Violent Cop* owes more to the stylish, hyper-realistic gangster films of Seijun Suzuki such as *Tokyo Drifter* and *Branded To Kill*.

Azuma is a cop on the edge – a figure familiar from the Clint Eastwood 'Dirty Harry' movies and all their imitators down to the 'Lethal Weapon' series – whose brutal methods get results. Unlike Eastwood's character, Azuma is not a justified

avenger or a vigilante with a badge. He's a functionary, a civil servant who bends the rules as casually as someone fiddling his expenses; but there's no sense that Azuma believes what he is doing is right.

At the start of the film, a group of delinquents harass and accidentally kill a tramp. Azuma passes by, sees what happened, follows one of the youths to his home, enters the house and beats him up, telling him to go and confess the next day. He does.

Azuma is quickly established as a maverick who is tolerated by his superiors. At one point after he has beaten up two drug dealers, his superiors collectively reprimand him; then, left alone with his commanding officer, he is told to write a mitigating report. "What sort?" he asks. "The usual," his commander replies.

In a series of increasingly violent scenes, Azuma goes head to head with Kiyohiro, a cold and sadistic yakuza assassin who, it is hinted, is like a criminal mirror-image of Azuma. The cops and the criminals are just two rival gangs, two establishments whose members will cross over and betray their own side for money. The film makes the point that the cops

その男、凶暴につき

監督■主演／ビートたけし

製作／奥山和由

配給／松竹富士株式会社

are dirty; the head of the vice squad has a deal going with the gangsters. Azuma plants dope on Kiyohiro as an excuse to take him and interrogate him, which results in his dismissal from the police force. Azuma, at least, is not motivated by money.

Kiyohiro then has Azuma's sister kidnapped where she is shot full of dope and gang raped by his henchmen. Azuma buys an illegal gun and searches out the gang for a final, cathartic shoot out.

Violent Cop is a comparatively fast-paced action film in comparison to his later work, though there are some of the familiar Takeshi touches that foreshadow what is to come. In a scene where Azuma interrogates a dope dealer in the toilet of a bar, slapping him and questioning him, the director stretches the scene out to an uncomfortable length, using the repetition to an almost comic effect.

He breaks some of the rules of conventional film making; normally, films always start scenes as close to their end as possible. Takeshi stretches them out, often cutting them before the point is made. It's clear because it's a technique he uses a lot, that it is for effect, not out of ignorance of film-making. Takeshi Kitano never set out with any burning ambition to become a film director — at least, he

won't admit that he did — and directed *Violent Cop* by accident when the original director dropped out. Takeshi, who was playing the lead role of Azuma, the violent cop of the title, had a six week window in his busy schedule and offered his services as director simply in order that the film would get made.

Violent Cop is a respectable thriller. Had he continued to make films like this, he would still be a name to reckon with. But he had grander ambitions and visions that couldn't be constrained by the rules; like Azuma, Takeshi was about to use unconventional methods to get results.

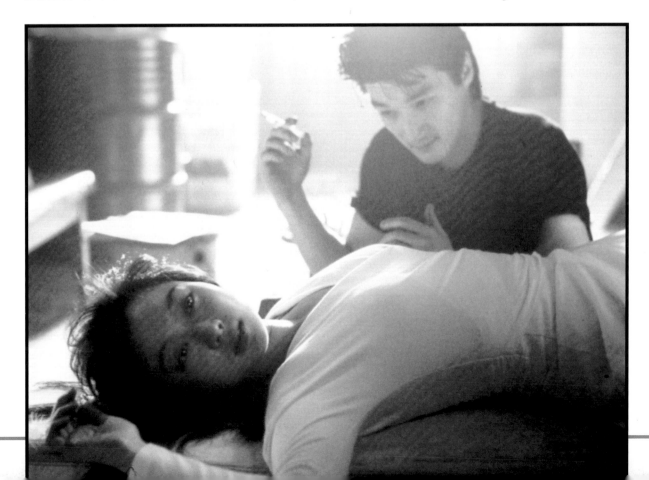

BOILING POINT

BOILING POINT (1990) 96 minutes
(3-4x JUGATSU/SAN TAI YON x JUGATSU)

PRODUCED BY: **Hisao Nabeshima, Masayuki Mori, Takio Yoshida**
DIRECTED AND WRITTEN BY: **Takeshi Kitano**
DIRECTOR OF PHOTOGRAPHY: **Katsumi Yanagishima**
CAST: **Masahiko Ono, Yuriko Ishida, Takahito Iguchi, Gadarukanaru Taka, Minoru Iizuka, Dankan, Makoto Ashikawa, Hisashi Ikawa, Beat Takeshi**

by Tommy Udo

If *Violent Cop* was Takeshi's apprenticeship in film, his sophomore effort *Boiling Point* is the work of a journeyman, delirious and possibly drunk with the possibilities of his medium. While *Violent Cop* is restrained, *Boiling Point* is the work of a man not so much testing boundaries as running headlong into them to see how far they will give.

It's his first work as auteur, where the film is his baby from start to finish. There's a sense that maybe he believed it would be the last film he would make, that he would be found out, so he had to cram as many ideas, as many images and as many of his personal visions into the film as he possibly could without any compromises.

He also wrote for himself the role of Uehara, one of the cinema's great human monsters, a gangster as fantastic, terrifying and unpredictable as Frank Booth (the unrestrained gas-sniffing psychopath as played by Dennis Hopper in David Lynch's *Blue Velvet*) or the supposed real-life yakuza assassin Rikio Ishikawa immortalised in Kinji Fukusaku's 1976 gory gangster epic *Death Of Honour* (released on video in the US in the mid 80s under the catchy title *Psycho Junkie*).

Unlike the nihilistic *Violent Cop*, *Boiling Point* has a moment of lyricism, telling the story of an innocent's confrontation with the underworld. Opening with a shot of the face of Masaki (Masahiko Ono) the film's main character sitting in a darkened toilet, he is immediately established as a bit slow, a simpleton when it's clear that he doesn't understand the basic and simple rules of baseball. The baseball team's coach Mr Iguchi treats him with patience and gets involved to help him when he insults a local yakuza at the garage where he works and runs foul of the gang.

When Mr. Iguchi is beaten up and hospitalised by the yakuza, Masaki volunteers to go to Okinawa to buy a gun and take on the gang in an act of bravado and stupidity. In Okinawa they meet

renegade yakuza Uehara (Takeshi) who has been ordered to pay back money he owes to the gang there and present them with the tip of one of his fingers, a customary yakuza way of showing atonement for wrongdoing. During his 20 minutes or so on screen, Takeshi's character casually smashes a bottle over the head of a man in a karaoke bar... twice; he makes his partner have sex with his friend while he watches then pushes him off her and sodomises him; he slaps his friend constantly in a manner that goes from slapstick to horror and back again. They casually kill an off duty American from the military base who has come to sell them weapons. Uehara and his partner go off on a suicidal attack on their local yakuza while Masaki and his friend take their guns and go home to do the same.

Boiling Point is actually constructed from a series of shots that look like still photographs. Faces stare impassively, occasionally moving or reacting, the camera held on them for what seems like an abnormally long time. The action is fast and brutal.

When a character is shot, it isn't lovingly filmed in slow motion as in a Sam Peckinpah movie. It's fast and ugly. Takeshi says that he grew up around yakuza and saw fights that were never longer than one punch. Apart from the prolonged and graphic shoot out between cop and gangster in *Violent Cop*, Takeshi's use of it is sparing, though usually messy and realistic.

He also employs some oddball comedy; while Masaki is on the beach in Okinawa, a man comes out of the grass with his trousers at his ankles, asks him if he has any tissue, then runs into the sea and starts wiping his bottom in the water. It's superfluous to the plot, the sort of detail that a mainstream Holywood movie would have cut at the script stage. Yet these touches add a real off-beat quality to *Boiling Point* that was missing from *Violent Cop*.

It's an ugly film about two characters reaching vicious boiling points, though Takeshi's ending makes us uncertain as to whether this is all Masaki's imagination simmering under his placid surface.

A SCENE AT THE SEA

A SCENE AT THE SEA (1991) 101 minutes (ANO NATSU, ICHIBAN SHIZUKANA UMI)
PRODUCED BY: **Masayuki Mori**
DIRECTED, WRITTEN AND EDITED BY: **Takeshi Kitano**
DIRECTOR OF PHOTOGRAPHY: **Katsumi Yanagishima**
MUSIC: **Joe Hisaishi**
CAST: **Kurodo Maki, Hiroko Oshima**

by Tommy Udo

Almost as a challenge to anyone who doubts his versatility, *A Scene At The Sea* – made between *Boiling Point* and *Sonatine* – is as far away from the rest of Takeshi's oeuvre as it is possible to get. No shoot outs, no yakuza hitmen, no existential cops, just a lot of warmth, humour and surfing.

The film centres around a garbage man who finds a broken surfboard, repairs it and splits his time between his friend and attempts to get to grips with riding the waves. It also becomes apparent during the course of the film that both are profoundly deaf, though it is hardly some big point that Takeshi is making.

It's perhaps the happiest of his films and probably the film with the least of himself in it. Despite being unable to hear one another, the boy and the man manage to communicate their love for each other. The surfing takes on a spiritual dimension, but it's hardly a great struggle with the elements. There's no tragedy, though the film isn't without moments of sadness, and no impending violence.

Just as all of his films foreshadow and refer to each other in some way – characters and images seem to resonate between them – there's some hint of the beach games scenes from *Sonatine* and an echo of the almost wordless relationship between Masaki and his friend from *Boiling Point*.

But this quiet, thoughtful film is the exception to all of Takeshi's other works, owing more to the introspection of French film maker Robert Bresson and perhaps to some of Takeshi's own short story writing, another facet to his creative output.

It's almost like another experiment, a page from a sketchbook where he tries out techniques that he'll later use to better effect elsewhere, still a film by a director learning about making films but nonthe – less enjoyable for being that.

SONATINE

SONATINE (1993) 94 MINUTES
PRODUCED BY: **Masayuki Mori, Takio Yoshida, Hisao Nabeshima**
DIRECTED, WRITTEN AND EDITED BY: **Takeshi Kitano**
DIRECTOR OF PHOTOGRAPHY: **Katsumi Yanagishima**
MUSIC: **Joe Hisaishi**
CAST: **Beat Takeshi, Aya Kokumai, Tetsu Watanabe, Masanobu Katsumura, Susumu Terashima, Ren Osugi**

by Tommy Udo

onatine is only a gangster movie in the same sense that Moby Dick is only a book about hunting whales and the Mona Lisa is only a painting of a woman with a wry smile on her face. By the time he made his fourth movie, Takeshi had grown in confidence as a director, as a writer and as an actor. *Violent Cop* and *Boiling Point* were both crime genre films. They were unconventional, certainly, but they did not step right outside of the conventions as Takeshi does in *Sonatine*. These first two films in particular were like preliminary experiments for his fourth.

The plot is simple and unremarkable enough: a group of yakuza are sent to Okinawa to sort out a dispute between two rival gang factions. Murakama (Takeshi) is their tired, possibly suicidal leader, who realises too late that he has been set up by his superiors. After a booby-trap in an office and a shoot out in a restaurant kills off members of his gang, he takes the survivors to a hide out in a deserted beach house.

Sonatine is the opposite of an action movie; it is, rather, an inaction film, punctuated by occasional rapid bursts of action.

Even after you see the film two or three times, however, the details of the narrative are lost in the emotional power of its central images; Murakama puts a gun to his head and pulls the trigger; a group of gangsters play a game on a beach, setting out a sumo ring and going through the graceful ritual motions but never engaging in a bout; the same gang play a war game on the beach with roman candles, prefiguring an apocalyptic shoot-out that goes on just a few seconds too long without showing anyone actually being killed – much of the shot is an exterior where we only see the fire illuminating a darkened room through a window –

upsetting all the conventions of the gangster movie.

It's almost as if, one hour into the film, he just stops the plot and plays around for a while.

Takeshi says that his screenplays are always constructed around a few central images that may or may not drive the plot along, an idea that would be anathema to the average market-research-led Hollywood screenwriter and corporate puppet directors. *Sonatine* is hardly an unapproachable, incomprehensible or self-indulgent 'art' film though in all fairness it did less trade at the box office than the films of his more plot, dialogue and action oriented contemporaries, directors Quentin Tarantino and John Woo.

But while critics have gone overboard describing the 'poetic imagery' and 'zen-like quality' of *Sonatine*, it remains a bitter revenge story, a theme that runs through several of

Takeshi's films. Murakama, exhausted by the violent world he lives in, contemplates and eventually becomes an avenging angel. There is also a lot of slapstick comedy that doesn't exactly deflate the darker side; it almost underscores it. When we first meet Murakama, he takes a man down to the docks, ties him up and dunks him up and down in the water, eventually drowning him. His nonchalance about violence is comical; this is Buster Keaton reincarnated as Michael Corleone.

Sonatine was not a commercial success when it was released in Japan. It was the first of Takeshi's films to get a wide release in the UK and in many ways it's a film whose precedents are in European cinema. Although the film got an American release – Quentin Tarantino's Rolling Thunder imprint distributed the film to a few selected arthouse cinemas – it was Europe that embraced Takeshi's work. *Sonatine*'s antecedents were films like *Mediterraniano*, about a group of Italian soldiers

stranded on an island playing football to relieve the boredom while they sit out World War II as well as the oblique early films of Jean Luc Godard such as *Breathless* (*A Bout de Souffle*).

Sonatine also provoked a confrontation between Takeshi and producer Kazuyoshi Okuyama who was alarmed at the way the film flouted convention and at one point threatened to take his name off the final credits. Takeshi also alleges that when *Sonatine* won a prize at the Taorima festival in Italy, his producers kept it a secret from him to try to rub in a sense of failure; it was only two years later at the Cannes Film Festival that he actually found out about the prize.

Although he professes that he feels no bitterness, his experience in making *Sonatine* – a film he so patently believed in – it strengthened his resolve to keep control of all aspects of his film-making in the future, launching his own independent production company.

GETTING ANY?

by Tommy Udo

GETTING ANY? (1994) 110 MINUTES (EXPORT CUT 76 MINUTES)
(MINNA YATTERUKA)
PRODUCER: MASAYUKI MORI, HISAO NABESHIMA, YASUSHI TSUGE,
TAKIO YOSHIDA
DIRECTED, WRITTEN AND EDITED BY: TAKESHI KITANO
DIRECTOR OF PHOTOGRAPHY: KATSUMI YANAGISHIMA
MUSIC PRODUCER: HIDEHIKO KOIKE
CAST: DANKAN, MOECO EZAWA, TOSHIO MIYAJI, HAKURYU, BEAT TAKESHI

The most atypical of all Takeshi's canon of film, *Getting Any?* is the Beat Takeshi familiar to Japanese TV audiences rather than European film buffs.

Tragedy is universal, but humour, like wine, doesn't always travel well and it will be interesting to see the reaction to *Getting Any?*'s forthcoming European release.

It could certainly blow Takeshi's art-film kudos in certain quarters, though you can't help thinking that that is something he would enjoy. *Getting Any?* is a crowd pleaser, packed with faces from Takeshi's 'army' or 'rat pack', revelling in bad puns, sick jokes and messy humour involving shit.

There is no real plot per se: *Getting Any?* is just a collection of shaggy dog stories linked by a character's quest to get laid. Asao is a socially inadequate loser who decides that he has to get a car to get laid.

He then goes through a series of more and more absurd schemes helped along by sitcom coincidences that are part Monty Python and fantasies that take us through movie parodies and pokes at Japanese culture.

Getting Any? sends up yakuza films – every so often a bleeding yakuza will drive up in a car, give Asao a gun or some drugs and tell him to look after it before dying – samurai films, Toho

studios monster movies, Japanese TV advertising, Michael Jackson's video for 'Beat It' and a 'Ghostbusters', in which Takeshi himself appears as a hyperactive mad scientist with a pudding-bowl haircut from the Japanese Invisibility Research Association who makes Asao invisible so that he can sneak into a women's bath house.

It's crude and faecal – when the character is transformed into a giant fly in a send up of films like

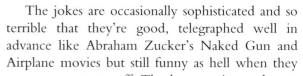

Mothra and TV shows like *Ultraman*, the scientists have to make the world's biggest turd to attract him by collecting shit from all over Japan – and a million light years away from *Sonatine*.

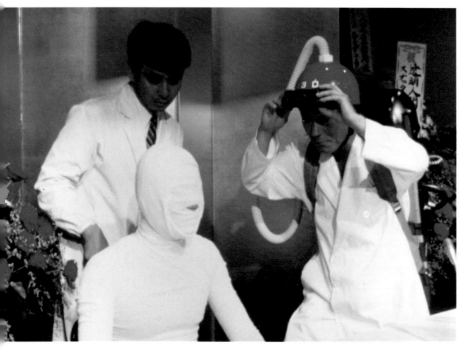

The jokes are occasionally sophisticated and so terrible that they're good, telegraphed well in advance like Abraham Zucker's Naked Gun and Airplane movies but still funny as hell when they come off. The humour is equal parts Monty Python, Benny Hill and The Three Stooges

But for all those film critics taken by the "zenlike" and "poetic imagery" of *Hana-Bi* or *Sonatine*, *Getting Any?* might be a little unsettling, like discovering that Derek Jarman also directed *Confessions Of A Window Cleaner*.

Maybe it's a reminder from Takeshi that while Eisenstein, DW Griffith and Abel Gance were making their masterpieces, the world's audiences were actually packing in to see Charlie Chaplin and Buster Keaton take pratfalls into trays of custard pies. It's also proof that while he's a hot serious director abroad, he's not above making people laugh by any means necessary.

KIDS RETURN

KIDS RETURN (1996) 108 MINUTES
PRODUCED BY: **Masayuki Mori, Yasushi Tsuge, Takio Yoshida**
DIRECTED, WRITTEN AND EDITED BY: **Takeshi Kitano**
DIRECTOR OF PHOTOGRAPHY: **Katsumi Yanagishima**
MUSIC: **Joe Hisaishi**
CAST: **Masanobu Ando, Ken Kaneko, Reo Morimoto, Hatsuo Yamaya, Mitsuko Oka, Ryo Ishibashi, Susumu Terashima**

by Tommy Udo

Following *Sonatine* and his critical success in Europe, Takeshi launched Office Kitano, his own independent production company, to make the films he wanted to make without interference from producers.

As a wealthy, successful TV personality, Takeshi had the luxury of not relying on his film career for a living and is thus able to be completely uncompromising about the films he makes without having to bow to commercial pressures.

But as if to confirm his status as a visionary, *Kids Return* became his most successful film in Japan, putting him on a stronger footing in the Japanese domestic cinema market as well as the prestigious (but not very lucrative) European and American arthouse circuits. There may have been a sympathy factor too: Takeshi's accident was big news in Japan and his recovery was tabloid fodder there akin to the latest doings of the Royal Family and Robbie Williams in the UK. Takeshi had planned to take a role in *Kids Return*, but was not well enough. It is the second film so far that that he has directed but not appeared in.

It's also one of his angriest and most autobiographical films. Although he's written books that deal with social issues, Takeshi's films are largely apolitical if anti-establishment.

In Japanese schools, children are often under intolerable pressures to succeed. Those who don't are often branded as failures for life when they are as young as 15 or 16.

The protagonists of *Kids Return* are Masaru and Shinji, the two class clowns in a below average Tokyo high school. Masaru and Shinji are both headed straight for the door marked failure. They spend their time distracting the swots, tormenting the teachers and extorting money from the other kids so that they can hang around in their favourite coffee shop all day. They're stupid but likable; rebellious without much of an idea what it is that

they're rebelling against. They start hanging around a gym and training; a washed up fighter takes the almost catatonic Shinji under his wing and teaches him the art of dirty fighting, illegal moves, drinking and gambling. The stupider but louder Masaru inveigles his way into the local yakuza.

There's an inevitability to the way that they screw up their lives; within a few years Shinji is already washed up like his mentor while Masaru has earned a punishment beating and expulsion from the mob. They meet by chance and Masaru asks Shinji if he thinks that their lives are already finished.

Takeshi, recovering from his accident and enjoying a second chance at life, would probably like to say 'no'. But he paints a bleak picture of a world where failure in youth is rewarded by a lifetime of exclusion. The characters are based on real people that Takeshi went to school with and makes the point that while they may not be finished, they will find that Japanese society is not really prepared to undo the mistakes they've made or make it particularly easy for them to achieve anything.

HANA-BI

HANA-BI (1997) 103 MINUTES
PRODUCED BY: **Masayuki Mori, Yasushi Tsuge, Takio Yoshida**
DIRECTED, WRITTEN AND EDITED BY: **Takeshi Kitano**
DIRECTOR OF PHOTOGRAPHY: **Hideo Yamamoto**
MUSIC: **Joe Hisaishi**
CAST: **Beat Takeshi, Kayoko Kishimoto, Ren Osugi, Susumu Terashima, Tetsu Watanabe**

by Tommy Udo

Although he started work on *Hana-Bi* before his accident, it is the film that is the most death-obsessed of all his works yet oddly it is also the most life-affirming.

It's almost like a 'remix' of *Sonatine* and *Violent Cop*; as if he's gone back to correct all the things that he was dissatisfied with in his previous films.

Nishi, Takeshi's character, is also a cop on the edge, like Azuma a haunted, existential anti-hero. Like most of Takeshi's characters, Nishi is barely better than the gangsters, a cold man capable of plunging chopsticks into a man's eyes with perfect calmness, or dishing out pointless and brutal beatings to juvenile delinquents.

Like Azuma with his sister, we only see a tender side to Nishi when he is with his terminally ill wife. For the first hour of the film, Nishi barely utters a word other than to grunt out a curt yes or no. Whether this is because of the accident – the whole right half of his face was paralysed and he was in a great deal of pain – or whether, as Takeshi insists, it was the way he scripted the character we will probably never know.

Nishi, an inspector in Tokyo's yakuza squad, leaves a stake out to visit his wife in hospital. While he is gone, his partner is gunned down leaving one cop dead and one paralysed. He becomes unhinged by the tragedy, going progressively out of control. He borrows money from a gangster, he quits the police force and holes up in a scrapyard where he plans a bank robbery using a fake police car.

Unlike *Sonatine*, the plot is complex. While Murakama was, like Nishi, sick of the world he inhabited, he had no way out other than suicide. Nishi, in his own way through the robbery, is at least attempting to deal with his dilemma and find an escape route. He tries to make amends for his past mistakes, by sending money to the widow and girlfriend of the cops, and sending artists materials to his wheelchair-bound colleague who always wanted to be a painter.

He takes his wife from the hospital on the road with him, trying to spend some quality time with her before death parts them.

But there's a doomed quality to Nishi, a dark and destructive side that will consume him and although his wife is dying from a terminal illness, he is also – call it his violent nature or his personal demons – and it is this evil that will kill him first.

Hana-Bi is an overwhelming experience; there is so much there, yet it is told fairly simply and quietly. As before, he creates scenes that are like still

> ...there's a doomed quality to Nishi, a dark and destructive side that will consume him

tableaux, punctuated by spurts of action. Often we do not see the actual, only its results. *Hana-Bi* is also an extraordinarily beautiful film to look at. Although he keeps control of writing, directing, editing and acting, you feel that if he could, he would also take care of the cinematography and the art direction too. As it is, in *Hana-Bi*, he did the paintings which play a huge part in the film's visual style.

The terms 'masterpiece' is overworked and devalued after being applied to everything from mediocre pop albums to forgettable plays, but *Hana-Bi* is unarguably a case where its use is justified. It isn't just a great Beat Takeshi film, a great Japanese film, a great cop film or a great film about death and dying. It's simply a great film, easily as good and as important as *The Godfather*, *Les Enfants du Paradis* or *The Seventh Seal*. It isn't a film like any other, its only precedents are

Takeshi's own films and puts him into a select elite of film-makers – Canada's Atom Egoyan, Britain's Peter Greenaway and America's Hal Hartley – who still make uncompromising films with a distinct authorial stamp, who stand apart from the mainstream conventions as to what a film should be and what stories they should tell. There's a saying that a writer should write about his or her life and times, because then they write for all people at all times. Perhaps it is because *Hana-Bi* is such an intensely personal film, it is therefore a universal story.

KIKUJIRO

KIKUJIRO (1999) 121 MINUTES
PRODUCERS: **Masayuki Mori, Takio Yoshida**
DIRECTED, WRITTEN AND EDITED BY: **Takeshi Kitano**
DIRECTOR OF PHOTOGRAPHY: **Katsumi Yanagishima**
MUSIC: **Joe Hisaishi**
CAST: **Beat Takeshi, Kayoko Kishimoto, Yusuke Sekiguchi,
Great Gidayu, Rakkyo Ide**

by Casio Abe

Takeshi Kitano completed the first phase of his career as a director with *Sonatine*, marking the arrival of a new phase with *Getting Any?* Even if *Boiling Point* was somewhat of an exception to the rule, this second phase is distinguished from the spare simplicity of the first phase by the complexity with which he puts together individual scenes, whilst still managing to maintain this overall simplicity. In a sense, this mirrors the history of cinema itself, which developed and grew through the discovery of new cinematic techniques. That's why it seems so fresh. By the way, as it were, scenes in *Getting Any?* that are reminiscent of the early days of silent films are built up like gags to create the story – this tribute to the earliest form of film being simultaneously realised through what seems like the re-enactment of a TV comedy. In the crueller *Kids Return*, parallel relationships between a number of lives are explored through an effectively compressed style – a more complex sensibility which is also not evident in his earlier work. With *Hana-Bi*, the fact that this is a work that points up 'parallel relations' is more important than the complexity vested in the shots. We can identify at least three of these here: the relationship between his own paintings and his screen images; between the value of life and death, and between love and melancholy. Moreover, in this second phase, Kitano begins to make efforts to define each aspect of the film with a comic touch, appropriately enough for someone who began his career as a comedian. His latest film, *Kikujiro*, is an extension of this process. In this work he manages to knit together the successful elements of his previous work and build something new as well. He is rediscovering where he has been, and at the same time breaking through to new ground. *Kikujiro* represents the high point of this process.

First reports of this film described it as a 'road movie' The gangster played by Takeshi happens to strike up a friendship with a young schoolboy, the plot involving them leaving Tokyo together so that he can take him to see his mother, during the course of which they travel all around

the country. The starting point is Takeshi's old stamping ground in Asakusa, but Takeshi's fastidious portrayal of the character of the area has no trace of sentimentality about it. He makes no attempt to show the various places that they travel to in a conventionally beautiful way, either. Featureless places – these seem to be his locations of choice. There is a tradition of setting movies in resort areas in Japan, but this film is about as far from that style as you can get. The places he shows are introduced piecemeal, but with a sense of dignity. This is his magic. Takeshi and the boy travel around Japan together in this way, but the film avoids being just another road movie. This is because he makes absolutely no use of smooth travelling shots to lure the audience in. This breaking with convention is typical of the film. There are many violent scenes, but the actual moment of violence is never shown (they break off half-way). It is interesting to note that although Takeshi is playing his usual gangster role, for the first time he plays a weak man. He is comprehensively beaten up by a gang of hoodlums at a local festival.

Although travelling with a child, Takeshi's basic attitude in this film is no different. He is as carefree as ever, and does what he wants. Despite that, though, eventually an emotional element creeps into his relationship with the boy. But this is not shown in a heavy-handed way. It probably only becomes obvious when we see how Takeshi tries to keep the boy from seeing that his mother now has another family, and is living quite happily with them. From then on, Takeshi, the boy and a group

of people they have met on the road start living rough in a place that can only be described as 'nowhere in particular'. The sequence of innocent games that they play there will be reminiscent of the Okinawa scenes in *Sonatine*. In the structure of the drama, Takeshi's role is to comfort the boy (like the character in *Hoshi Wo Tsugumono*). In an early scene of the film, Takeshi is deliberately shown to be a hopeless case. But later on, as he starts to feel himself again, he is able to acknowledge that in fact the child has comforted him. In the ancient folk society of Japan, it was thought that children are 'little gods' who have been sent to help adults. That's why although this is a film about 'healing', it is focused on the adults, not the child. This is revealing of Kitano's current state of mind, as is one other thing, which it has in common with his previous film: the appearance of an angel (and one of Takeshi's paintings). In his previous film, the angel was full of melancholy and a sense of abandonment, reminiscent somehow of Paul Klee or Walter Benjamin. But through its association with the 'little gods', the angel in this film is distinctly Japanese.

The 'Japanification' of this film is probably the key to understanding it. This is the reason why a more traditional folk element, represented by the hoodlums and buskers, is given a significant presence on screen. And although there are plenty of places which raise a laugh by building up a sequence of short gags, one should be aware that the laughs owe a great deal to the spirit of Asakusa

where he learnt his trade. The film is thus much more oriented toward more traditional comedy than the more light-entertainment style of *Getting Any?* This is, of course, a tendency evident in his career as a whole, and he is clearly going out on a limb with the introduction of the 'Asakusa' element into the film. There is a wonderful scene half-way through the film at a bus stop in a country area, the sort where buses never come. The character who appears with Takeshi in this scene is his old partner, Beat Kiyoshi (from the stand-up manzai duo, The Two Beats). The artists of the old Asakusa in the 1920's and 1930's, particularly in its glory days, were all trying to emulate Charlie Chaplin. In so far as this film is recreating something of that old-time ambience, it is quite natural that one should think of Chaplin, but in fact this conceals Kitano's ultimate coup. He is not following Chaplin. Though busy introducing Chaplinesque moments, he is always planning an escape. Even in the small details like a laugh that fades away, it is pure intention on Kitano's part.

In any case, whether it be this 'Asakusa' laugh, the succession of folkloric moments, or the fact that the relationship between the gangster and the boy is mutually comforting, not just a one-way street, the complex sensibility of this film makes itself evident. One more thing worth paying attention to is the number of scenes that stand out from the overall flow of the narrative. For example, the scene where a pervert played by the avant-garde dancer Akaji Maro appears as a frightening presence in the boy's dream. Or the scene shot through a distorted glass, like the view through a dragonfly's compound eye. Or the imaginary scene where a tengu (a key figure in Japanese folklore, rather like a cross between a bird and a monk) appears at a shrine. For some reason, though, these scenes blend naturally into the rhythm of the film. Of course, abrupt comic moments are often incorporated in a film to alleviate a state of tension. But Kitano has amply demonstrated that a film can still work with a continuous flow of inconsistent images in *Hana-Bi*, through his use of paintings.

The film starts out from Asakusa, and comes to an end there once more. It is a movement that traces both a circle and the number zero. There is a precedent for this, of course, in *Kids Return*. The outburst of emotion, the affection and warmth as the circle is closed is also familiar. But in this film the character that Takeshi plays does not reveal his name until the final moment. When the little boy suddenly asks him his name, Takeshi replies *Kikujiro*. It is the name of his own father. One can see, then, that the character he plays must bear more than a passing resemblance to his father. The humanity of this effort to reach back into his past is not lost on the audience, and gives a sufficient reason for the tears that flow

Ryuichi Sakamoto

David Bowie

Nagisa Ohshima
MERRY CHRISTMAS MR. LAWRENCE

戦場のメリークリスマス

●監督 大島 渚 ●製作 ジェレミー・トーマス
●脚本 大島 渚＋ポール・マイヤーズバーグ ●原作 サー・ローレンス・ヴァン・デル・ポスト
●撮影監督 成島東一郎 ●美術監督 戸田重昌
●音楽 坂本龍一

何をしでかすか、
大島軍団！
新たなる感動を目指して
ゴー！

デビッド・ボウイ、坂本龍一、ビート・たけし、トム・コンティ、ジャック・トンプソン
大島 渚プロダクション、テレビ朝日、レコーデッド・ピクチャー、シネベンチャー提携作品
イーストマン カラー、ドルビー・ステレオ 松竹・富士映画共同配給

■■ DOLBY STEREO

Takeshi

Tom Conti

[映像]

MERRY CHRISTMAS MR. LAWRENCE

A Culture Clash Against the Background of a POW Camp

by Tommy Udo

Merry Christmas, Mr Lawrence is a remarkable film; a rare Anglo Japanese co-production, it teamed Nagisa Oshima, one of Japan's most uncompromising directors, with a cast of western and Japanese actors and non professionals playing out a drama of culture clash and attraction against the background of a prison camp in Java in 1943.

As a director, Oshima will always be remembered for *Ai No Corrida* (*In the Realm of the Senses*), a film that is still shocking over 20 years after its first release. Like *Merry Christmas, Mr. Lawrence*, it was set against the background of the war, though the major world events were only glimpsed briefly as the film bored deeply into the painful, violent and dark tale of a couple who literally decide to fuck themselves to death.

If he had a European counterpart it would perhaps be the doomed German meister film-maker Rainer Werner Fassbinder; that an Oshima film would venture from the con-fines of art-house cinemas to High Street Odeons was in itself an amazing feat.

As well as casting the then movie virgin Takeshi in one of the pivotal roles, the choice of Ryuchi Sakamoto – then launching a solo career after a spell in Yellow Magic Orchestra, one of Japan's major domestic and export electronic pop bands – and David Bowie – then enjoying one of his periodic flushes of creativity – guaranteed ticket sales in Japan and the UK and the US.

While Sakamoto's Captain Yonoi and Bowie's Major Jack Celliers played out the conflict that drove the film – between the harsh Samurai code of honour and the charismatic Celliers' own personal unyielding rebellion – Takeshi's character Hara and Tom Conti's Mr Lawrence also play against each other. Lawrence is an outcast, mistrusted by the other POWs and misunderstood by the Japanese guards and commandant, while Hara is confused inside by the friendship he feels for him. The arrival of Celliers upsets any kind of equilibrium – however brutal – that has been established between guards and prisoners.

The Japanese regard everyone as lacking in honour. They regard the prisoners as dishonourable for being taken alive and they regard themselves as having been dishonoured, guarding them rather than fighting for the Emperor.

Hara feels that Celliers should have killed himself rather than be taken prisoner and becomes torn between resentment and fascination at a man that the others so obviously regard as a hero. Takeshi subverts the character of Hara who fits some of the *Bridge On The River Kwai* stereotypes of the brutal, bullet-headed Japanese prison guard, bringing a sense of loneliness and confusion of a man far from home.

Merry Christmas, Mr. Lawrence was one of the first (and only) films to present Western audiences with a perspective on the war from the Japanese point of view, a subject that can still arouse great bitterness from surviving inmates of the POW camps. For everyone involved, it may not be anyone's best film – Oshima, Bowie, Conti, Sakamoto or certainly

Takeshi's – but it's still a remarkable and courageous film when viewed 16 years on.

Nagisa Oshima, one of Japan's most respected directors, has worked in the film industry for nearly 40 years. We speak to the director of *Merry Christmas, Mr. Lawrence* about the inspiration behind the casting of a relatively unknown up-and-coming comedian in a major film.

Jeremy Thomas is one of the few international producers, if not the only one, working in the British film industry. He talks about the problems of cultural communication both on and off screen in *Merry Christmas, Mr. Lawrence*.

Respected stage actor Tom Conti has been a mainstay of quality British TV drama for years and is known to audiences for films as diverse as *Shirley Valentine* and *Reuben Reuben* (for which he was nominated for an Oscar). Here he talks about filming with Beat Takeshi and the difficulty of playing a Japanese-speaking character when he himself cannot actually understand what he's saying.

INTERVIEW WITH NAGISA OSHIMA
by Yuki Sato

Q: Why did you get Takeshi involved in the film world?
A: Unlike most directors, I find it frustrating to have to cast only actors. I'm always on the look out for people from a different field. Although I didn't think about Takeshi specifically in that sense, I had a gut feeling that he had natural acting ability, having worked with him in the past on several TV variety shows. In fact, I think it was during one of those shows that I asked him if he fancied acting in a film. He said straight away that he was a bit shy about it, you know the way that he is. I urged him to do it and gave him two pieces of advice. The first was not to settle for a minor role. I told him to go for a big part right from the start. The second

was not to appear in a comedy, simply because he was already well known as a comedian. But, at that time, I wasn't planning to ask him to take a part in one of my own films. It was just a general question, to find out whether or not he was interested in acting. Even when I first started work on *Merry Christmas, Mr. Lawrence* – which I had a lot of difficulties in casting – I never dreamed about asking Takeshi to get involved.

Q: Describe the process that led from your initial conversation with Takeshi to you casting him in Merry Christmas, Mr. Lawrence?
A: Oh, it just came to me like a divine revelation!

Q: You cast not only Takeshi, but also Ryuichi Sakamoto. Nowadays, it's fairly common for directors to use other professionals in their films. In fact, many have followed your example. At that time, however, it must have taken real courage to cast both a comedian and a musician. Did you think of them as a sort of combination?

A: Initially, I only looked at Takeshi and his role. After casting him, I decided on Sakamoto without even meeting him. What happened was that I saw his portrait in a photo book called *Fifty Representative Figures of Today*, or something like that, in which I was also featured. I stared at it for ages, then suddenly I just knew that I wanted him too. I said to myself, 'OK, that's it!' Then I wrote to him.

Q: Although you got a great cast, wasn't it hard to teach them how to act?

A: I was confident that both would do well, even though neither had any acting experience. In Takeshi's case, I didn't have any difficulties at all. Although he wasn't an actor, he is an entertainer, and so he had a sense of how to perform.

Q: Among the many impressive scenes in the film, perhaps the most moving is the last scene with Takeshi and Tom Conti.

A: Oh, yes. When we were making the film, there were several scenes in which everyone cried. The morning after we shot the last scene, all the make-up artists appeared on set with their hair shaved off, which is what Takeshi had to do for his role. We were all very moved.

Q: During the shoot, did Takeshi show any signs that he would become the film director Takeshi Kitano we know now? Did he bombard you with a list of questions? Did you see any evidence at all of his interest in directing, as opposed to just acting?

A: No, it was quite the opposite. He didn't ask any questions. He simply turned up on set as a person who played the role described in the script. When he stood in front of the camera, he was completely immersed in his role. He wasn't Beat Takeshi anymore. There was no time to spare for any extra conversation, nor was there any need for it.

Oshima with Tom Conti

> In Takeshi's case, I didn't have any difficulties at all. Although he wasn't an actor, he is an entertainer, and so he had a sense of how to perform

Takeshi's acting was beyond my expectation. It was obvious that he had a very strong presence.

Q: Why is it that you seek out non-professional actors from other fields?
A: I simply don't like established methods. There are six billion people on this planet, but I'm supposed to choose someone after looking through just 20 or 30 actors' portraits. I've felt the same way since the beginning of my film career. And if I do things differently, perhaps I can stretch the horizons of my work. It's something I think about every time I make a film.

Q: Presumably, that's also the case with your latest film, Gohatto?
A: I always want to encounter something new, not just in casting. This time, I set out to make a film which I knew would require a lot of effort after a long break from the business. It was a fresh start for me, so naturally I wanted to find new performers.

Q: So it's the circumstances in which the film is made that dictate what you do?
A: As far as I'm concerned, I simply find my next project, then write a script. It's that script which opens up all the possibilities.

Q: With Merry Christmas, Mr. Lawrence, did you imagine making a film of the story when you first read the original novel, The Seed and the Sower by Laurens van der Post? What's the difference between a book which you want to turn into a film and a book which you just flick through, then forget about?
A: Oh, it's simply intuition, don't you think? Or maybe it's inspiration. In the case of van der Post's novel, it grabbed me the second I started reading it, or even before I started. I found it by chance in a book shop and read the blurb on the dust jacket. It said something like, 'The encounter of an English officer and an aggressive Japanese warrior in a Japanese POW Camp in Java.' After reading only those words, I thought that it might make a hit film.

Q: Even ordinary people sometimes visualise certain scenes when they read a novel. Which particular scene did you visualise when you first read The Seed and the Sower?
A: As you could probably guess, it was the scene right at the end, where Takeshi's character says, 'Merry Christmas, Mr. Lawrence.' The whole film

A: To do their job, musicians use their bodies as instruments. They regard their bodies as instruments. In short, I think that they are able to play certain tunes through their bodies.

Q: So are there certain similarities between entertainers and musicians? Or do they have a different way of expressing themselves?
A: I think they are similar. Entertainers also express some sort of tune by using their bodies. It may not be music, but I think they express melodies or rhythms.

Q: After Takeshi was highly praised for his performance in Merry Christmas, Mr. Lawrence, he played the serial rapist and murderer Kiyoshi Okubo. Now, he has a reputation as an actor of some ability. Judging by his film history, he seems to seek the dark side of life, which is very different from how we see him in his comic performances. Did you spot that side of his nature even when he was a comedian?
A: Yes, I did. That's one of the reasons I advised him to play a villain. I could see that he had a dark side to him even when he was playing a comic role. That was the main reason I cast him for Merry Christmas, Mr. Lawrence. I could sense that he had something different about him, something which ordinary people can't express.

works towards that. We shot that scene on an island. It was really hard work, but it's what I remember most about the film. There were loads of people there. One thing I'll never forget was when David Bowie arrived on the island and said, "Oh, I see, we're going to be prisoners of Oshima for the next two months." When he said that, I thought he had grasped the theme of the film itself and the true nature of film-making.

Q: Why do you think that musicians – for example, Bowie and Sakamoto – are so good at acting?

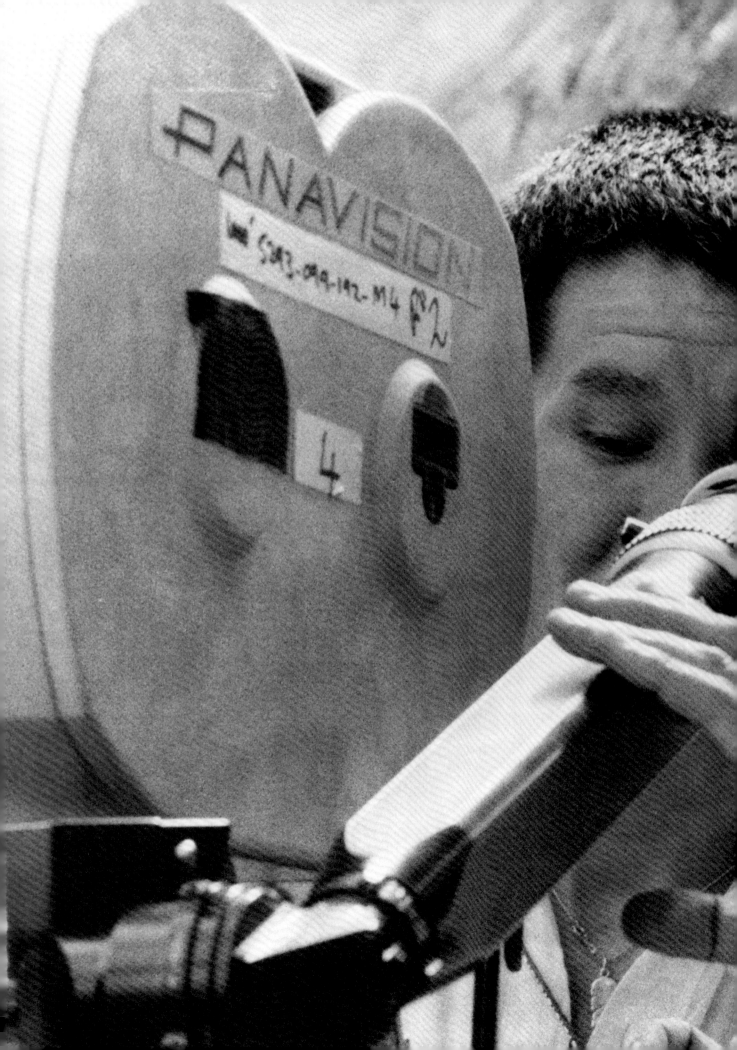

RIGHT TO LEFT **Oshima, Tom Conti, David Bowie**

Q: About Merry Christmas, Mr. Lawrence, the English actor Jeremy Irons said, "I was asked to play the role which Tom Conti later took. I rejected it because the screenplay contained a strong sign of homosexuality. But the film was wonderful, and I deeply regret that I turned it down." Do experienced actors like him often make such misreadings?

A: Well, I can only suppose that he didn't know who the director was. I'm joking, of course. But seriously, had he been Japanese, he would have known what kind of director I am. It would have been hard for a foreigner to understand. David Bowie, however, had seen some of my previous films and was able to say that his favourite was *Death by Hanging* (*Koshi Kei*). But I think that is odd for a foreigner. And Bowie is odd.

Q: How did you contact David Bowie? Did you ask Jeremy Thomas for help?

A: I just contacted him on my own. I said, "Please do it!" Jeremy wasn't involved at all. I can't remember what Bowie was doing at the time. He may have been appearing in a commercial for a Japanese liquor, or something like that. So I suppose I asked one of the crew for a contact for his agent. Then I just wrote him a letter.

Q: Recently, there has been a lot of talk about the positive attitude of actresses such as Nicole Kidman, who directly contacted the film director she wanted to work with. Do you see yourself as the pioneer of this?

A: I don't always act so speedily, but in Bowie's case I had to. If I hadn't done it, it wouldn't have happened. So I wrote to him myself, and he took up my offer. He said straight away that he wanted me to come and see him, so at least I knew that he was interested. That said, it must have been easy for him to say, "Okay, come and see me." It was harder for me even to buy a plane ticket.

Q: So you flew to see him. Did you get positive feedback right from the start?

A: Yes, although I think that creating something is like climbing up a ladder, step by step.

Q: *After Merry Christmas, Mr. Lawrence got great reviews, Takeshi embarked on a career as a film director with Violent Cop. Did he ask you to see that film?*

A: No, he didn't. But of course I saw it. And I thought that he had the natural sense of a director rather than simply the ability. He had his own natural sense. I thought that there is a sort of film in the world which only he could make.

Q: *You mean that Takeshi is the type of person who instinctively knows what he wants to film?*

A: I think so. Or I could say that he has something which he wants to express physically.

Q: *Takeshi went on to make several films. They were critically acclaimed, but they weren't very popular with the general public in Japan. How do you evaluate his films in terms of his natural ability and his progress as a director?*

A: That's a difficult question. I don't know if he has made any progress or not. I've never even thought about which of his films is my favourite. I like them all. I suppose his talent might match mine. So even if I sometimes think that he has made a mistake, I still see him working in his own style, which includes those mistakes.

Q: *Have you thought about asking him to act in your next film, Gohatto?*

A: I already have. He has agreed to play the role of the Samurai hero, Toshizo Hijikata. He fitted me into his schedule.

Q: *That's a wonderful surprise! Takeshi playing Hijikata sounds so sexy. It's something no-one would think of. When did you first come up with the idea?*

A: I had it in my mind from the beginning, when I was writing the screenplay. Takeshi said that his

schedule was tight, but it was the same situation with *Merry Christmas, Mr. Lawrence*. For that film, I put together the schedule on my own, after an absence of some ten years.

Q: *Can you imagine how he will play Hijikata?*

A: I imagine it will be his own interpretation, put it that way.

Q: *Takeshi has lost a lot of weight since Merry Christmas, Mr. Lawrence. He also had a terrible accident. He has acquired quite a threatening presence these days, don't you think?*

A: The hardest parts to cast in this film were the roles of Hijikata and Isami Kondo. The problem was that both those characters are 'leaders of men'. And actors are not like this. They are 'lone wolves'. Takeshi, however, does fit into that mould. That's why his participation is essential.

The hardest parts to cast in this film were the roles of Hijikata and Isami Kondo.

Q: *When did you first notice Takeshi's talent for directing?*

A: When he became popular as part of the double act The Two Beats. He was unusual.

Q: *What did you think of Violent Cop? Did you feel that something was missing from that film?*

A: In *Violent Cop*, you could see Takeshi's strengths so clearly. As his career as a director has developed, his work has become deeper and more meaningful. The longer he goes on, the deeper his films become. He has been at it for ten years now, during which time he had the accident and coped with a lot of problems. I think those experiences helped to give his films depth. His early films were more direct, as mine were too. That's only natural. Depth only comes through experiencing – experience of shooting several films and of life itself. It's a combination of both. Also, every director learns a lot from the crew and actors they work with.

Q: *When you look back on Merry Christmas, Mr. Lawrence, what's the first thing that springs to mind?*

A: The people I met. When I made *Ai No Corrida* (*In the Realm of the Senses*) in 1980, I got used to associating with non-Japanese. So when I was shooting *Merry Christmas, Mr. Lawrence* and *Max Mon Amour*, I wasn't particularly conscious of the crew as a whole or of the foreign locations. What I really remember was meeting people on an individual basis. That said, I was aware that, having worked abroad so much, I was keen to return to Japan for my next project.

Q: Even if you do return to Japan, European audiences will still be keen to see your next film.
A: I do love being abroad. When I collapsed in London a few years ago, I remember thinking that if I was to die now, it would have been quite cool!

Q: Takeshi has said that foreign journalists are very knowledgeable. Have you ever been surprised by questions you've been asked by journalists from France or Britain or wherever?
A: Oh, I'm continuously surprised. Because I was something of a pioneer, I had to take on the responsibility for questions about Japan itself. I was considered to be the only person who represented both contemporary Japan and the world as a whole. I knew that was why I was always asked so many questions. I had to give my opinion on so many issues. That was a real experience for me, and it taught me a lot.

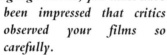

UN FILM DE **NAGISA OSHIMA**

Q: Considering the language barrier, you must have been impressed that critics observed your films so carefully.
A: Absolutely. I was very impressed. For example, someone said to me, "In your films, there is always glaring sun. But in *Nippon-Shunka-Ko*, it changed to the black and white rising sun flag, fluttering in the wind. What does that symbolise? Does it indicate a change in Japan?" I managed to get round the question, but I'll

"MERRY CHRISTMAS MR. LAWRENCE"
A FILM BY **NAGISA OSHIMA**

never forget the face of the person who asked it. Also, I was often asked what my aim was in making films. I always wanted to answer, "That's none of your business. Leave me alone." Instead, I'd just say, "In order to understand myself." Once, somebody replied, "You don't need to make 35mm wide-screen films to understand yourself. You only need a black and white 16mm film for that!" You know what I replied? "I use colour 35mm wide-screen in order to understand myself, and because I'm such a splendid director!"

Q: Nobody would mind if a film made specifically for the Japanese market was released only in Japan. But it's good publicity if a film gets a worldwide release, so many are thrown together by TV companies targeting foreign film festivals. What do you think when you see that happening?
A: I think, 'Let them just get on with it.' Maybe they'll learn something from it. They will find out what it's all about eventually. If they don't see anything wrong in what they're doing, that's their problem.

Q: What are your favourite recent films?
A: I liked *Hana-Bi* a lot. Also, *Inu-Hoeru* by Yoichi Sai [who is to take the role of Isami Kondo in Oshima's *Gohatto*] and *Moe-no-Suzaku* by Naomi Sendo. As for foreign films, I like the work of Abbas Kiarostami, who I met once, and the Russian director Aleksandr Sokurov.

Q: What do films mean to you?
A: I knew that I was the sort of person who wanted to express something, so it was a happy accident that I fell into films.

Q: And we are a lot happier as a result.
A: I hope so. Audiences get the enjoyment. Film makers have to deal with all the difficulties.

Q: Takeshi once said, 'I hate those film kids who have been carrying a camera since the day they were born and making some sort of movie with it'. Have you ever felt like that?
A: Takeshi also said, "I want to experience a lot of things and reflect them in a film which swings like a pendulum." I don't have the same ability that he

has to do both films and comedy equally well. In fact, I joined the film industry in order to eat. But I share the same sentiment in that I don't want to be seen as an idiot who can only make films. I always think about whether or not my life is going in the right direction. In short, I'm an arrogant person! I wanted to do something better with my life than what I was born to.

Q: Films often are the driving force of your life, rather than a means of self-affirmation?
A: Yes. I always think, 'This is no joke'. I observe people. I suppose that I have more of a curiosity about human beings than the average person. As I get older, I have become more aware that I have a spirit of perversity. I know that I should cast ordinary, clean-cut actors in my films, but I can't.

Q: Any final comments?
A: Making *Merry Christmas, Mr. Lawrence*, I had many happy experiences and some difficulties. Now, I truly enjoy being able to talk about Takeshi and the film itself. Honestly.

INTERVIEW WITH JEREMY THOMAS
by Takato Imai

Q: How did you get involved with Merry Christmas, Mr. Lawrence?
A: I met Oshima at Cannes in 1978. It was the year that his *Empire of Passion* (*Ai No Borei*) won the Best Director award. *The Shout*, which was a film I produced, directed by Jerzy Skolimowski, won the Grand Prix. I sat next to Oshima at the prize-giving dinner and we exchanged business cards, as you do. Then a couple of years later, I received this project from him via an intermediary called Michiyo Yoshizaki, who was a representative of Herald Ace in London at the time. I read the screenplay that Nagisa had

written and then I read Laurens van der Post's book and decided that I would do the film. I thought it could be brilliant. I had to go to Japan anyway because my film *Bad Timing*, directed by Nicholas Roeg, was being released by Herald Ace. I went to Tokyo first and met with Oshima to talk about the possible production of the film.

Q: For the casting, is it true that Oshima relied on you to choose the English cast, while he chose all the Japanese actors?
A: We had discussions about the screenplay and

Jeremy Thomas with Tom Conti, Takeshi, Jack Thompson

Mr. Paul Mayersberg – who wrote *The Man Who Fell To Earth* and *Eureka* – was employed to do a small adaptation of Oshima's script. That worked well and it was that screenplay which was then presented to various people. Of course, Oshima had already settled on several elements of the film, including the casting of Sakamoto and Takeshi Kitano. David Bowie was also just about to come on board, then Tom Conti was cast after Nagisa saw him audition in London. Tom was very strong, a consummate actor and incredibly generous with all the other actors, including Takeshi. I think he helped the non-actors a lot because he's a brilliant technician. He had problems learning his Japanese lines, but even so he went out of his way to help everyone else. You can see that in the movie.

Q: Tom Conti said that although this was the first time Takeshi had acted a big role in a film, he could tell that he was a natural actor.
A: He was exceptionally good. The only real problems were with his time schedule. He had to travel back and forth to Rarotonga, which included a trip via Fiji or Auckland. He had to do that twice. Even in those days, Takeshi was phenomenally busy.

Q: It's obvious that you are a courageous film-maker, always setting trends and staying several steps ahead of everyone else in the film world. Even now, Merry Christmas, Mr. Lawrence looks very modern and particularly appealing to young people. At the time, you must have been incredibly brave to use people like Ryuichi Sakamoto who had no acting experience.
A: I've always been very involved in youth culture. I still am. So I knew who Sakamoto was because of Yellow Magic Orchestra. Then I discovered Takeshi and totally understood what he was about. When I look at *Merry Christmas, Mr. Lawrence* now, I can see that it was very innovative from a production standpoint. We made the film in Rarotonga, in the New Zealand area, in order to get money from the New Zealand council. It was a genuine co-production with them – as much a cultural co-production as a business co-production. I knew the script would make for a great film as soon as I read it. I'd seen lots of prisoner-of-war movies made by English people, but it was fascinating for me to see a master Japanese director make a film about a prisoner-of-war camp. Considering the time which has passed between World War II and today, to have a radical, brilliant

master of cinema make a film based on Laurens van der Post's book was amazing. That's what initially interested me in the film. Of course, there were other aspects of it that I loved. The culture, for a start. And David Bowie. As an actor, I think it's probably the best thing he has ever done. And Takeshi made an outstanding debut. His performance moved people to tears.

Q: When Merry Christmas, Mr. Lawrence was screened at the Cannes film festival, there were rumours that it would win the Palme d'Or and that Takeshi and Tom Conti would win prizes as best actors. But they received nothing. Were you disappointed?

A: No, not disappointed. I was just happy that the film was included in the competition. I was delighted with the success we had in selling the film and getting people to distribute it. I wasn't really thinking about winning prizes. It would have been nice, but we got our reward anyway because we made a wonderful film. There may have been some confusion about that prize in Japan, because another Japanese film won that year (In 1983 *The Ballad of Narayama/Narayama Bushiko* by Shohei Imamura won the Palme d'Or). But it didn't bother me that we didn't win. I was very happy with the result. In fact, I've never expected to win any prize, not even for *The Last Emperor*, which got an Oscar. I don't make the sort of films that tend to win awards. But it is nice, occasionally, to be recognised for your work. I know Oshima felt the same way. He wasn't competing as an artist. It was the media that made out there was some sort of conflict going on. There wasn't. Everyone likes to be a winner, but artists don't compete against each other. It's incredibly difficult to judge a piece of art, and therefore it doesn't matter so much when you don't win a prize.

Q: What is your favourite scene from Merry Christmas, Mr. Lawrence, particularly of those involving Takeshi?

> **Everyone likes to be a winner, but artists don't compete against each other.**

A: I like the scene between Takeshi and Tom Conti, where one says to the other, 'I'd like you better if you killed yourself' meaning, 'I'd respect you more if you committed hara-kiri'. That scene sums up all the confusion between both men. They respect each other, they think they're both good men, but they can't understand how it's possible to be a prisoner and a proud man at the same time. The implication is that you'd kill yourself if you were a prisoner. Tom Conti's response to that would be, 'Ah, that's a coward's way out. We don't believe in that. We want to fight and to go on fighting, but we want to do it in a different way.' Therefore, there is a dramatic, cultural conflict of politics and ideology in just that one scene. That's why it's so stimulating for me. Of course, it really is a Japanese film made in English. It's not like a European film at all. Its a very pure Japanese film, but the language just happens to be English. A British film maker wouldn't approach it in anything like the same way. That's what makes the film unique.

Q: Were you on set for the shooting?
A: I was there every day. I didn't leave the island while the film was being made. I was there when we shot in New Zealand as well, and outside Auckland.

Q: Tom Conti thought everything was done on Rarotonga.
A: It wasn't, although I don't think he was in any of the scenes shot in Auckland. The scenes with the little boy, the younger brother of Bowie, and the bit where Bowie was taken to the military trial in Batavia (now Jakarta) were set in Auckland railway station and nearby. We obviously designed the place to look like the Batavia headquarters.

Q: Do you have any interesting anecdotes about Takeshi?
A: Not that I'd be prepared to talk about.

Q: Did he tell a lot of jokes?
A: He was very good company. It was odd us all

being stuck on a South Sea desert island which has a population of only a few hundred people and just one restaurant, and a few desert palms. It was a very unusual, very intense place to make a movie.

Q: What were your impressions of Takeshi as an actor?
A: He was just a great guy. What you see with him is what you get. He's a fantastic artist. You could tell he was absolutely enjoying what he was doing and totally in control of it. He's an unusual person. I can't think of any equivalent artists, certainly not in my country. And you can't really think of many other places where that type of person could exist, where they could be taken credibly as an actor, a comedian, a writer and a film director.

Q: Did Takeshi mention at the time that he would like to make films?
A: No, there was no indication at all that he was going to become a great movie director. Although I'm sure he got the smell of a movie set from that film. It was a very intense time for all of us. I guarantee that anyone you interview about that film will say that it was a highlight of their career. It was a really enjoyable movie to make and we got a very satisfying response to it from all over the world. It was a perfect lesson in film making.

Q: Have you seen many of Takeshi's films?
A: Yes, lots of them.

Q: What did you think?
A: He's a wonderful film director, very natural, just as he is a natural actor. I loved both *Sonatine* and *Hana-Bi* and I enjoyed *Kids Return*. I like most of the films of his that I've seen. They're all so original. They're good, strong examples of modern Japanese cinema.

Q: They're not necessarily huge hits, but people always pay attention to his films.
A: Takeshi gets a lot of respect because his films are both unusual and good, which is a rare combination today. I'm sure he'll go on to make many more great movies.

Q: Some people say there's too much violence in his films

A: I don't agree. Over the years, there has been all sorts of great film-makers. Sam Peckinpah, for example, was a master of violence, and he has made some of my favourite films ever. So clearly there is room for poetic violence in cinema.

Q: About his colours – it is often noted that Takeshi loves blue, he calls it Kitano Blue?
A: I haven't analysed his films that much. Different people have different forms of film criticism, but Takeshi is making the films in a free style and what comes out is natural work. He shoots in a natural way, not a preconceived way. That's what makes his films original. It's a very healthy way to work.

Q: As an actor, he says he's hungry. Do you think many directors would be keen to use him?
A: I'm not sure. I'm only really aware of his films and of his growing international reputation. Of course, I've known him on a personal level since I worked with him many years ago. But I'm sure that if he wants to do something, he'll do it. He could certainly become a big star abroad. He could achieve what Roberto Benigni has, for example.

Q: Oshima is to make a new film soon. Do you have any thoughts on that?
A: I'm looking forward to seeing his film. He's a great master.

Q: Many people worry about the state of Japanese cinema when a wonderful director like him couldn't make a film for a long time in Japan.
A: The situation is difficult right now. I'm sure it will get better. I've seen some good Japanese movies recently and it is a great cinema of the world – and the second largest market in the world. These things go in cycles.

Q: How would you change the film world? Your directorial debut All The Little Animals appeared to be a low-budget project, yet it had so much in it. Are directing and producing two totally different disciplines?
A: I produce so many films. I was going to be a director. Before I was a producer, I was an editor. I produced and edited my first film, then I got stuck

for 20 years producing movies. Suddenly I thought, 'I must direct this film.' With *All The Little Animals*, I found a story that I wanted to tell. And I had a wonderful time last year making it, so I definitely want to do it again. I just wish I hadn't waited so long. It was a personal film, a film about things that I love, like nature and animals. I could comment on so many things, plus there was a sort of thriller/dramatic background to it. It was a real departure for me. I thought that if Takeshi could act, direct, write, stand on stage and attempt lots of different things, then I too should take up a challenge.

Q: What was the budget of that film?
A: Not much – £3 million, which is about $5 million.

Q: Did the actors work for less because of you?
A: No, I only had John Hurt and Christian Bale, but they're not superstars, just good actors, wonderful actors in fact. The film got a great reaction. It went down well at the London Film Festival, in Tokyo, at Cannes, Toronto, San Sebastian. We've been everywhere with it and it has been very enjoyable.

Q: What is your next project as a producer?
A: I'm going make a medium-to-big-budget film with Bertolucci, set in the Renaissance period. It's about a composer.

Q: You were involved in The Brave. The story is that Johnny Depp couldn't get any Americans to invest in the film, then he happened to see you at Cannes and approached you about it. Is that true?
A: We just met and he said, "I want you to do this film with me." I said, "Okay," and found the money. I liked the script. I still do, although I don't think the film was given a proper chance. There was too much hysteria around it. It was good for a first-time director. People want films to be too much like other films. It's a very original piece of work and it was incredibly brave of him to make it.

Q: When The Brave opened in Japan, it got a good reaction. What do you see as the future for the film

form, because people's tastes are obviously changing.
A: Although it is a very difficult time at the moment, I'll just continue doing what I've always done, which is find a story that I like and make it with a group of people that I enjoy working with. You're right that the industry is changing a lot, but I've been going for 25 years now and I think I can continue on my own track because, regardless of the delivery system, people will always want stories told in a good, unusual way. As you said, I'm known for creating my own vision, for following my own instincts, and that's what I'll always aim to do. Sometimes I win, sometimes I don't. In the long term though, it must have worked in my favour because most of my films are still popular today.

Q: *Can box office sales be a problem at first?*
A: DVD has helped. People want to see all of Bertolucci's films, all of Skolimowski's films, all of Nicholas Roeg's films, all of Stephen Frears' films and all of Cronenberg's films. People will want to watch films by great filmmakers forever. I hope that, in the long run, I'll fall into that category. I think that DVD will be the saviour of international cinema. It will make art-house films widely available, because they don't get shown on TV. Foreign language films have a hard time getting even cinema distribution. But if people can choose to watch them themselves, a whole new market will open up. We just have to wait for the unit price of DVDs to fall low enough, to around the price of a ticket to a cinema – 8 bucks, maybe 10 bucks. In Britain, for example, there are almost no outlets for Japanese films at the moment. You can't get a sub-titled Japanese film shown in the cinemas or even on Channel 4. But when the films are available to buy for £5, I'm sure the market will change. The film business needs ancillary markets

to pay for itself. Studios rely on an income from sources such as TV, DVD, video and merchandising to support and promote the film theatrically.

Q: What about art-house cinema?
A: It's definitely in the doldrums at the moment. It's going through change.

Q: Especially in England.
A: That's because we're dominated by American companies, which only want American films to be shown in England. We're locked in a business war at the moment.

Q: Can you fight back?
A: Not really. I'm trying to do it my own way. But I need American studios too. They have only one objective, which is to make profits. That is their business. We have to find a way of working with them, which means a way of making profits for them.

Q: Do you still keep in touch with Takeshi?
A: I saw him at the London Film Festival and at the Tokyo Film Festival. He started to be accepted in the film world with *Merry Christmas, Mr. Lawrence.* He's well known in Europe by people who understand what's going on in popular culture around the world.

★Jeremy Thomas announced he would produce Takeshi's next film, *Brother*, soon after this interview.

INTERVIEW WITH TOM CONTI
by Takako Imai

Q: Merry Christmas, Mr. Lawrence was Takeshi's film debut. Until then, everyone thought of him as a comedian.
A: I was told he was a comedian and that at the time he was doing 11 hours of television every week in Japan. But as soon as we began shooting the film, I knew that the man was an actor. You can tell immediately if someone is truly an actor or not. I knew that Takeshi was not only an actor, but that he was a great actor, which of course he has since proved himself to be.

Q: You and Takeshi worked well together in the film. How did you get involved?
A: I was approached in the usual way. The producer called my agent and sent over a script. I read it, liked it and agreed to do the movie. It was a little odd because I didn't meet Oshima, the director. He just trusted Jeremy Thomas, the producer, to find the right actor for Lawrence, which turned out to be me. My first scene in the film was with Takeshi and my first speech was in Japanese. I spent a whole week – all day, every day – with the language coach, who was a Jew from New York, not Japanese. His name was Roger Halbers and he was the most amazing linguist: he could speak Russian, Japanese and probably French as well as English. I'd walk up and down the beach with him while he taught me all my Japanese lines. On the first morning, I was very nervous. Takeshi may have been nervous too because it was his first scene in a big movie, but he didn't show it. He seemed very calm. The scene went fine. There was a good relationship in the story between Lawrence and Sergeant Hara , and somehow that affected our own relationship. I was

sorry that I couldn't talk properly to Takeshi because he didn't speak any English and I didn't speak any Japanese. It sounded as though I spoke Japanese, but I didn't really. I enjoyed all the scenes with Takeshi. They were probably my favourite parts of the movie because there was a real connection between us.

Q: Did Takeshi tell jokes to the cast and crew?

A: I have no idea because he always spoke in Japanese, but he did make the crew laugh a lot. It's great when an actor or a star takes time on set to entertain the crew. It makes everything go so much more easily. Takeshi was a bit of a clown — he would clown around and occasionally, I would join in with him. So it was good fun. The last scene in the movie, when Sergeant Hara is about to be executed, was very emotional and Takeshi was

wonderful in that, truly wonderful. It's one of the best pieces of acting I've ever seen. He was able to go from this hard, bullying, cruel man whom we had seen all the way through the movie to someone who suddenly changed to a compassionate person, quietly awaiting his death.

Q: How many times did you rehearse that scene?

A: Not many. Once or twice, maybe. You don't rehearse much on film. Also, Oshima liked to use the first take. In the West, directors waste a lot of film and often the first take is bad. The actors always try to get it right from the start, but quite often the crew are not up to speed. The first take for the actors will be good, but the microphone boom will come in or maybe the focus will go soft, so you have to do it again. Sometimes, actors need four or five takes to get back to what they had on the first take. That's very irritating. It also wastes a lot of film. But in the West, nobody cares about wasting film because it's cheap. In Japan, directors don't think like that. They never waste film, so everyone is prepared for the first take – the technicians, the cameramen, the sound guys, everyone. And Oshima made sure that they all knew the rule – you aim to get the first take absolutely right. So almost every scene in the movie is a first take, which is truly remarkable. It shows the skill of the actors, particularly Takeshi, who was able to get it right straight away, despite the fact that he was not trained as an actor.

Q: Do some actors think it's better to repeat scenes again and again?
A: Definitely. I've never talked about this to an actor who has only done movies, but shooting a scene is a bit like performing in front of a live audience because there are 60 or 70 people standing round all watching, i.e. the crew. Certainly, if you're stage-trained, you automatically embrace that audience. If the scene isn't right, you can feel it because the crew become bored, they're looking around. But if it is working, everybody's watching, and so you sense that too.

Q: Rumour has it that Takeshi and Ryuichi Sakamoto got on very well, but that David Bowie, who was already a big star, was very distant.
A: No, he was just the same as everyone else. David is a very hard-working man. He takes his work seriously. I remember one awful morning when David was feeling sick, and he had to be buried up to the neck in the scene we were shooting. What he was most afraid of was that he was going to throw up, because he couldn't bend over, he had to stand up straight. He had a terrible time that day, but in general, he was a good friend on that film.

Q: What about Ryuichi Sakamoto? Someone said that his acting in the film was bad, but that it had a fresh feeling. He's not trained as an actor.
A: No, he's not. And a lot of the time he was required to speak English. It's incredibly difficult to act in a foreign language. You don't really understand most of what you're saying. I knew

what I was saying in Japanese, but I didn't know what it felt like to say it as a Japanese person, which is a different thing. So I had no idea whether I sounded good or awful when I was speaking Japanese. I just had to rely on luck and hope that the director would say something if it was really bad.

Q: You just memorised the phrases?
A: Yes. I still remember them all. The learning process was so intense that I've never forgotten my lines. It's strange and this was 1983, a long time ago now. My brain is the only muscle I have that works well because it's the only one I ever exercise. All my other muscles are no good.

Q: Oshima trusts Jeremy Thomas, but did you respect Oshima?
A: Oh yes. I didn't know him, but I had seen one of his films, *Ai No Corrida*. In the script, there was a love scene between me and a girl, in bed. So when I watched *Ai No Corrida*, I thought, 'Oh my god, what will he want me to do?' I was afraid he'd want a very graphic sex scene and I don't like to do that on screen. I also felt sorry for the poor girl. She arrived on set at 8 o'clock in the morning and an hour later, she was naked in bed with me. I didn't know her and she didn't know me. It was a strange situation, having to do explicit sexual stuff together. I was worried about her. Anyway, we both spoke to Oshima about it, and he said, "What do you want to do?" We said, "Well, we'll just do it normally!" – what we call in Britain the missionary position. She said, "Um, um, um – nothing special, no acrobatics." So we were lucky there. Then after all that worry, the scene didn't even make the final cut.

Q: So was she your girlfriend or a prostitute?
A: She was a girlfriend, a woman my character met on the morning of the fall of Singapore to the Japanese. It was love at first sight. The two went straight to bed, then never saw each other again.

Q: Many people thought the film might have won at Cannes. Takeshi thought so too. And he thought that you and he would get actors' awards too. But he

won nothing. He was angry about it. He talked a lot about that on TV and radio. Did you fly to Cannes to promote the film?

A: Yes, I did. I was only in Cannes for one Sunday because I was in a play in London at the time. David was there. I remember there was a story that someone had died, and everyone thought that person should get the prize. Maybe Takeshi was going to get a prize and suddenly it went the other way because this man died and everyone said, "Oh we should give him the prize because he's dead." A prize is no good to you when you're dead; its only useful when you're alive. It's so stupid.

Q: You didn't win anything either.

A: No. There are only two movies I've ever won anything for out of twenty that I've been in. It doesn't happen often. There's only one award that really makes any difference though, and that's an Oscar, an Academy Award. That's the only award that's worth anything in the movie business.

Q: Did you hear the result while you were in Cannes?

A: No, that comes at the very end and I was there for a day in the middle. I didn't see anything. You go from the airport to a hotel room and you just sit there while journalists come in one after the other. Maybe you get to go to the beach for lunch, but usually you have to give interviews there too. Then you get in a car and go back to the airport. So you don't have fun, you don't have any time to meet girls, nothing. You just talk to journalists, then go home.

That said, I loved being involved with anything to do with the film. I was talking to Jeremy about a month ago and we both agreed that *Merry Christmas, Mr. Lawrence* was an experience which we'll always remember. It was a very special time. It was extraordinary to be on that island, with the part-English, part-New Zealanders, part-Japanese crew and actors. The difference in cultures was amazing, the location was exotic and the subject

> **The learning process was so intense that I've never forgotten my lines.**

matter very special. It was a big thing for all of us who took part in it.

Q: Where was the location?

A: A little island called Rarotonga, about 1500 miles from northern New Zealand, in the middle of the Pacific Ocean. We built the concentration camp on the island.

Q: Shooting was hard work, but when you had time off, could you enjoy life on the island?

A: Yes, it was nice. There was a great beach. We were all a bit scared about sharks though, because it's the Pacific Ocean. Swimming was always a little nerve-wracking. But it was the kind of desert island that people dream of, really beautiful. There was one tragedy during the shooting – a Japanese crew member disappeared and was never found. We don't know what happened to him. His wife came down. It was very sad. Apparently, there was some problem with her state pension because his body was never found. Japanese law says that you have to be missing for 25 years before the wife is officially declared a widow and is allowed state help. We were all very concerned for her. It was awful. He hadn't been well and was suffering from depression, and when he didn't come to work, he lost face and didn't want to come back. It was all very complicated. A real tragedy.

Q: How long did shooting last?

A: I can't remember. A couple of months, I think, but it was so long ago. I remember certain bits, but not how long I was on the island. Then, towards the end of shooting, my wife called to say she had found a lump on her breast. She had just discovered it that day. So I flew back to England and the shooting had to be rearranged. It turned out to be a benign cyst, so I went back. There are many reasons that I'll never forget that movie.

Q: Takeshi speaks very little English, but could you converse with him at all at that time?

A: It was very difficult. I do remember laughing quite a lot with him though. I knew he was a serious man. But most comics are serious people. Generally, they're not that funny in real life because comedy is a serious business. It was extraordinary when I went to see *Hana-Bi*. It's a phenomenal movie. There's an amazing mixture of lyricism and hardcore violence. It's very interesting that Japan has so little violence in its society. It's much safer to walk through Tokyo than it is to walk through London. Nowadays, you can't let a child out on its own in this country, anywhere, not ever, because it's so dangerous. Yet in Japanese movies like *Hana-Bi*, there is an amazing amount of violence. You wonder if the Japanese are violent or if they are just fascinated by violence. His painting is amazing, really beautiful. I didn't know he paints, because I didn't see him doing that during the shooting of *Merry Christmas, Mr. Lawrence*. Maybe he did in private.

Q: He did a lot of painting when he was recovering from his motorbike accident.
A: That was tragic, really terrible. I noticed in *Hana-Bi* that his face had been damaged. It gave him a real Clint Eastwood-like quality. He says only five words in the whole film. Mostly he says, "Hmm, hmm." It can't have taken long to learn the dialogue, which is good. That's the kind of movie to make. You can go drinking the night before, then go home to bed and learn your lines the next day. He writes the script, so he can give all the dialogue to the other actors. But that's common for big stars. They don't like to do a lot of the talking. If you go and see a movie with Steve McQueen or Clint Eastwood, they hardly ever speak. They look and they know, but they don't open their mouths much.

Q: You saw Violent Cop, Sonatine, Boiling Point and Hana-Bi. Were they the same?
A: You can see a change in style. *Hana-Bi* is very sparse. It's like a Japanese garden.

Q: Could you imagine Takeshi making a film when you first met him?
A: Nothing surprises me in this business. If you'd asked me at the time if I thought Takeshi would remain a comedian, I would have said no. I thought that he would get more involved in movies, but I didn't know if it would be directing or writing them. I was certain that he would continue to act though. Film is an amazing art form. As Orson Welles said, "It's the best train set a boy ever had." What all boys want is an electric model train set, and a movie set is like a bigger version of that. It's the best toy you can have, the ultimate toy. Boys like toys.

Q: Do you want to make a film?
A: There's a movie I've been trying to make for years. It's set in 1938. I get closer and closer and suddenly something happens and it all falls to pieces again.

Q: Is it a good time to make films in England?
A: No, not really. There's no money in Britain for movies, or at least very little. You can only make very small movies here. If I could make this movie for $2 million, then I make it tomorrow, but at $6.4 million, it's proving very hard to produce. That's the figure I'm aiming for. I suppose one day I'll get it made.

Q: Since Merry Christmas, Mr. Lawrence, have you worked with any Japanese actors?
A: No, unfortunately not. I always hoped that someone might invite me to Japan to make a movie, but no-one ever has.

Q: Out of film and theatre work, which do you do most?
A: About half and half. Theatre work can be very lucrative. If the show's successful, I make a lot of money. Of course, it can also be dreadful, in which case I get nothing at all. Most people don't make much money in the theatre, but a few of us do, maybe only four of us. If you're famous and are cast in a leading role in a West End play, then you get a good wage. It's hard to make a fortune from it though. Most of the money I make is from screen work. I just made three bad movies. I didn't make them bad, but they were bad, which is always annoying. They looked okay on paper, so they should have been good!

ALL ABOUT TAKESHI'S MOTHER AND HIS MISDEMEANOURS

In his career Takeshi has twice faced momentous crises. The first came in 1986, when he was 39 years old. This event was triggered by a photo scoop in the weekly scandal magazine Friday, which ran a report on his close girlfriend, saying she was his mistress. Takeshi wouldn't tolerate this attack on his private life, so leading his Gundan – his army of faithful followers – they raided Friday's editorial offices, beating up and threatening the staff and trashing the office. The police arrested Takeshi and his Gundan, but though they were soon released, Takeshi decided he needed some time out and took a seven months break from work.

Friday had got the story from a man claiming to be a freelance journalist, who began hanging out with Takeshi after promising to place articles in well known magazines. Takeshi gradually realised this man was leaking details of his private life to Friday, which made him even more angry. He couldn't stand his privacy being revealed in such a devious way. He could take attacks on himself and his own life, but he said he couldn't ignore the pain inflicted on somebody else, someone not in the public eye. Following the attack on Friday he was

prepared to be banned from television work, and became seriously concerned how this would affect the lives of the Gundan involved in the raid. He was ready to accept the public's judgement and punishment but their reaction was unexpected. After his comeback he was voted top TV celebrity in an NHK (Japanese TV) popularity poll and appeared on many TV programmes.

Despite this, he felt a growing disillusionment with the TV world, typified by the aimless style of programme which shows viewers how to cook food instantly in a microwave oven. He fancied making a film, if somebody could be found to give him a chance.

The opportunity was to come very soon, and quite unexpectedly. In 1989 at the age 42, Beat Takeshi became the film director, Takeshi Kitano. Just before shooting began on the film *Violent Cop* starring Takeshi, the director Kinji Fukasaku decided to quit the project. Production company, Shochiku Fuji, decided to use Takeshi as the director as well as the film's main character. This seemed to be a publicity stunt and Takeshi accepted his new job lightheartedly. He wasn't so keen to make the film and during a press conference Takeshi nervously admitted, "I regret now that I accepted it. Anyhow I'll do my best. But directing is a wonderful job, because no one else can complain about my acting. Whether I'm a genius or not, I certainly won't make an ordinary film."

Violent Cop won a prize at the Japanese Academy Awards in 1990, and during the awards ceremony everyone was surprised to see Takeshi dressed in a brightly coloured kimono, clothes traditionally worn by young unmarried girls. The media was very interested in the film, but it wasn't so well received by the public. At the time nobody believed Takeshi would make a serious filmmaker. Many assumed his assistant directors had made it and expected this would be the beginning and the end of his movie making career. In fact until *Hana-Bi*, none of his films were hits inside Japan. To most Japanese he was a comedian and a TV personality. People who admired his films at this early stage were foreign journalists and critics such as Tony Rayns. Takeshi still appreciates Tony's support and recently said, "Tony found me first!". Tony Rayns powerfully spread Takeshi's reputation, showing his films in the U.K., the first time outside Japan, in cooperation with Simon Field, former ICA Director of Cinema. European cinema fans had already discovered him to be a stylish filmmaker. This support helped give Takeshi the freedom to follow his own artistic direction in his films. His vision and methods are slightly different from other Japanese feature film directors. He doesn't operate on huge budgets, but refuses to shoot when unhappy with a set or location. When *Sonatine* began shooting, to protect his artistic freedom Takeshi clashed with Kazuyoshi Okuyama, producer and head of Shochiku Fuji. Okuyama expressed his anger against Takeshi, accusing him in a magazine interview. He vowed Takeshi would never make another film. Nevertheless, *Sonatine* was officially screened at Cannes, appearing in the Un Certain Regard category. The film was highly acclaimed but Takeshi was the only participating director who didn't support his film at the festival. Ironically Takeshi grew bigger as a film director after splitting from Okuyama, whose own problems grew when he was forced to quit Shochiku Fuji with his father. On the day the news broke, Takeshi ironically joked, "Today is his funeral day."

After Takeshi completed *Sonatine*, he gradually became disillusioned with his career, including TV work. The Gundan, Takeshi's army, always addressed him as 'Tono' (My Lord), and one member recalled, "Tono kept repeating the words, 'I want to die' when he was drunk, or dreamt up ways to die and end his life." He might have felt some limitations as a comedian. Just before his motorbike accident, it was reported he was dating the actress Fumie Hosokawa. The rumour mill pruriently suggested, 'Is she his new girlfriend?' Takeshi completely denied the rumour. "She is a very charming girl", he insisted, "We don't have such a relationship." Despite this distraction their friendship survived and Takeshi cast her in his film *Kikujiro*.

In the dead of night on 2 August, 1994, in Shinjuku Ward, Tokyo, Takeshi took a right hand bend too fast on his brand new motorbike, lost control of the machine and smashed into a barrier. Unconscious and seriously injured he was taken to the intensive care unit of a local hospital. His injuries were a fracture on the right side of the skull, a brain contusion and a complicated fracture of the right cheek bone. The Japanese press reported constantly on Takeshi's condition and were fascinated as to why such a thing had happened.

Takeshi completely lost his memory of the events either side of the crash. Hardly anyone believed he could survive or make a full recovery with such severe head injuries. "Maybe I tried to kill myself. I remember drinking a little bit of alcohol, but I don't remember why I had to ride on a motorcycle. Was I going to see one of my girlfriends? I can't remember at all."

For the first week after the accident he said it was like living in a dream world. He imagined seeing a stuffed doll of Beat Takeshi thrown up in the air and falling violently on the ground. He picked up the doll and it was empty, its head and face completely smashed. He also confessed to being annoyed by press reports which continued to invade his privacy.

To squash these rumours he held a press conference, and in a magazine article wrote that he wanted to die before reaching fifty as he didn't want to become a worn out old stager. He admitted that many things had put him under pressure, tension and strain before the accident, many elements that led him to suicidal action. Yet he didn't die in the accident. Luckily there was no intracerebral haemorrhage. A doctor said this was almost a miracle. His face was now a big contrast: the left side was perfectly normal, but the right, especially around the eye, was severely deformed. He had an operation to rebuild the dented cheek bone. His condition improved daily, but he found difficulty speaking properly and he couldn't hold a cigarette between his lips. The wrinkles, lines and expressions disappeared from the right side of his face. He was suffering from facial paralysis and his doctors ordered brain surgery to regain his facial movement, but he firmly refused. He used his instincts, his sixth sense, to decide what was best. Many people questioned his decision and doubted how Takeshi could survive as a performer in the harsh world of television with such a facial disability. From his hospital bed Takeshi watched many films and videos including works by Akira Kurosawa and Francis Ford Coppola. He worked on the plot of a very violent movie, to the surprise of many people. On 26 September, 1994 Takeshi was finally discharged from hospital. Next day he appeared in front of the media pack at a press conference. Takeshi's paralysed face painfully contorted in reaction to the flashes of the still cameras and the heat of the TV lights. He kept on repeating to himself, "I have to cope with my face, I will cope with this paralysed face."

For Saki, Takeshi's mother, he was always a big baby boy. Saki's jokes, with their black sense of humour, were very similar to her son's. She encouraged him with words like, "You should die, idiot!" In her first hospital visit after the motorcycle accident, she berated him, "If you die in an accident, you should die in a Porsche car, like James Dean, not on such a small motorbike." Although her words seemed gravely unsympathetic, she went to a shrine near her house everyday to pray for his full recovery. Saki always supported her youngest son in her own inimitable way.

In 1987, after the existence of his mistress was revealed in a scandal magazine, his beloved wife, Mikiko, declared she would get a divorce, leaving Takeshi very upset and depressed. Saki told some journalists, "I would like to advise my son's wife to grab as much money as she can from him in compensation." In reality she was strongly against their separation and encouraged them to get back together again. And so they did!

1987 was a year full of ups and downs for Takeshi. He finally decided to leave Ota Productions, which had managed him since his days in The Two Beats and later as Beat Takeshi, to set up his own film production company, Office Kitano. The following year Masayuki Mori, who used to work with Takeshi as a TV director, joined

Office Kitano, becoming managing director in 1992. Since Mr. Mori joined Office Kitano, he has used his skills as a film producer to guide Takeshi in the right direction. Mr. Mori encouraged Takeshi when he hesitated, and calmed him when he became too excited.

When we look back at Saki's past, she did not have an easy life. Her mother died soon after she was born and at the age of thirteen, when her family fell on hard times, she was forced to go up to Tokyo and enter service with a wealthy family. They were very happy with her because she was such a hard worker, even for someone so young, and they treated her like a member of the family. Ushi, a shamisen teacher who gave private lessons to the daughter of the household, adored Saki and arranged a marriage to her son, but he died tragically shortly before the wedding. Instead Ushi adopted her as a daughter and made her marry her nephew, Kikujiro, Takeshi's father. Kikujiro was a very lazy man, he didn't enjoy his work as a painter and was always drunk and violent. Saki kept on working very hard to save money to educate the children. "Why did I do that? The poor can only escape from poverty through good education." But Takeshi tried to escape from her scheme by dropping out of university and leaving the family home. After Takeshi became a comedian, she was always watched him nervously in front of the TV worrying in case he made a mistake. When Takeshi called her from Venice with the news that he'd won the Golden Lion Award with *Hana-Bi*, Saki responded in her usual way. "You got gold? How big is it? How much is it? Can I use it in my gold teeth?"

His vision and methods are slightly different from other Japanese feature film directors

But then she began to cry with happiness. At the end of 1998, Saki unfortunately broke her left leg and was admitted to hospital. It was very difficult to recover from the injury because of her age. She gradually became weaker and weaker until she couldn't eat and speak properly. In his new film *Kikujiro*, Takeshi suddenly decided to insert a scene where Kikujiro goes to see his mother in hospital. His thoughts often went out to her. She was hospitalised far from Tokyo, and with so much TV work to complete Takeshi couldn't get to see her very often. On 22 August, 1999 Saki died peacefully. She was 95 years old. When Takeshi went to see her two weeks before her death, he called out, "Ma, Ma, Ma!" She didn't reply but Takeshi knew, "I'm sure she recognised me because she was staring at me. I know she was very old, but she was my mother. I feel that I've lost something." Takeshi had eight or nine weekly TV shows but he cancelled them all for three days, to stay and comfort her soul. The purple coffin made especially for her was surrounded by a sea of white flowers. Many Japanese celebrities and Takeshi's fans attended the vigil and the funeral. Even Japanese Prime Minister, Keizo Obuchi sent a wreath of flowers. Before a throng of about a hundred journalists, Takeshi was too sad and downhearted to crack his usual jokes. "I always watched my mother working so very hard and crying. I can never thank her enough. I told her 'I will be a greater man. I will try my best to do better work. I want to be a better boy, Ma!' " Takeshi kept on crying with tears, like a little boy. Outside the rain was falling heavily and there were some peals of thunder.

Takeshi directs Kids Return, his first film after his motorbike accident. He went to Cannes to promote this film

Takeshi Returns With Kids Return

by Yuki Sato

A nervous Takeshi Kitano was close to tears. It was night at the Cannes Film Festival. Takeshi's sixth film, *Kids Return*, had been selected from more than 200 films from all over the world to be screened during the Directors' Fortnight and had got a great response. "As a stand-up comedian, I am used to performing in front of an audience and I never feel nervous," said Takeshi, the day after the screening. "But when I had to get up on stage to introduce my film, it was a different story. I started shaking as soon as I heard the applause. I thought I would make people laugh by pretending to stumble when I walked up on stage. I tried it, but it didn't work. Instead, the audience just went silent, which made me more nervous. I wasn't even sure what I was going to say. I'd had nightmares about it." The applause from the audience in Cannes was not for Beat Takeshi, the comedian, but for Takeshi Kitano, the film director. Although clearly exhausted from giving 40 interviews to foreign journalists during his stay in Cannes, Takeshi still managed to crack a joke about his schedule. "As I was going between the room, the terrace and my hotel roof for interviews and photo-sessions," he said, "all I could think was, 'What am I – a pigeon?'"

In Cannes, audiences are notoriously hard to please. Critics often leave cinemas in the middle of a screening if a film has failed to impress them. The sound of people leaving their seats must be unbearable for a director. "To be honest," admitted Takeshi, "I think I would have died if people had got up to leave. I had a feeling it was going to be okay though when I heard everyone laughing at the scene where the two main characters suspend a doll from the rooftop. The doll is supposed to resemble their teacher – with his penis out."

On the set of Kids Return

Kids Return is a tale is about two high-school drop-outs. One is trying to become a professional boxer, while the other wants to join the Yakuza, the Japanese equivalent of the mafia. One of the important characters in the film is a guy called Hayashi, who is struggling for survival as a boxer. He not only offers devilish advice, but also introduces the two kids to booze, cigarettes and even drugs. "Hayashi himself was once a junior champion boxer, but then he failed to make it to the next level," explained Takeshi. "The suggestion is that he gets jealous when he sees a youngster as strong as he once was and decides to lead him on the same road to failure that he wound up on.

"I saw the same thing happen in the world of stand-up comedy. When I was a young comedian in Asakusa and had just started to do well, there were several people who tried to hold me back.

ABOVE AND BELOW Kids Return

They would say, 'It's easy to be funny if you're any good at comedy.' Whenever I said I thought I should go home and work on my gags, they'd tell me, 'You don't have to work hard if you have talent. Let's just get drunk and have fun instead.' So that's what I would do. One night, I went out drinking with them, then the next morning, I went straight to NHK (a Japanese TV station) and I got punished for it. They banned me for an entire year!"

At Cannes, the film's ending threw up an interesting contrast of views. After going through a series of bizarre events in both of their lives, the two kids ponder their future. One says, "I wonder if it's all over for us now." The other replies, "No, we haven't even started yet." European journalists perceived this as a negative message, while Japanese journalists saw it as positive. "I didn't know what to think when one journalist from Japan told me that that line cheered him up," said Takeshi. "To me, there is certainly some melancholy attached to that ending. The two kids are saying that although their lives are not over, they know that their future doesn't hold much hope. That's sad. I think it's a

> **To be honest I would have died if people had got up to leave**

very Japanese trait to attach some romanticism to it. The romance of knowing you've blown it, but being prepared to give it one last shot anyway. You've hit the bottom and you know there's no way out, but yet you keep on trying. The more you try, the deeper you go down. But the Japanese see a virtue in persistence. Again, I experienced something similar when I was in Asakusa. Someone told me, 'You don't need to be on TV if you are already a successful comedian here. To live and die as a comedian in Asakusa, that's a beautiful thing. Isn't that what you wanted when you came here in the first place? You left college, you failed in the students' movement and you had no idea what to do or where to go. Where did you find a place to call home? Wasn't that here in Asakusa? And yet now you want to leave.'

"Being content with what you've got is a very Japanese way of thinking and I quite like it." So was it a feeling of melancholy rather than sadness that the film was expressing? Certainly, it managed to capture the ambition and energy of youth, albeit short-lived. "In the place where I grew up, there was a lot of poverty. Many people were born poor and died poor. Some say that's a sign of no hope. But I'd say, 'Have you ever had something in your life that made you happy that has nothing to do with money?' You might have had fun with a bloke next to you at the bar on a night out on cheap whiskies. In my opinion, no one lives and dies with nothing. There are moments in everyone's life which really shine."

In Takeshi's film *Sonatine,* there is a scene in which a group of Yakuza make a trip to Okinawa. In the bus on the way to the city from the airport, a person welcoming the group says, "We have cold drinks and ice cream for your refreshment." It was another example of a scene which provoked a mixed reaction from audiences. Some found it funny, some didn't. "I was actually hoping people would find that scene funny. No matter how tense a situation is, there is always a moment where we can't help but laugh.

"I had a call from the family of a friend called Itsumi, a famous TV personality in Japan, who was

OVERLEAF **Boiling Point**

Violent Cop

on his deathbed. They wanted me to see him before he passed away. It's terribly hard to go and see a person knowing he is going to die. You can't help but cry. So do you know what I did when I went to see him in hospital? I cracked jokes non-stop for 30 minutes. The pair of us just laughed our heads off. And I know our minds went blank at one point and that was the best thing."

Sometimes, when we know a situation is hopeless, we can't do anything but laugh. Asked about this in relation to the comedy element in his films, Takeshi gave the following reply. "I totally agree with that notion," he said. "And it doesn't really matter if laughter seems inappropriate in certain situations. When we have a good laugh, we go blank. I think that's what comedy is all about and that's what people are looking for when they go to see comedy. We know that comedy can help us forget all the worries in our lives. And things can be even funnier when we are in a situation where we are not supposed to laugh, for example when someone farts at a funeral. That's a killer!"

In Japan, Takeshi is recognised as a man of many talents. In Europe, his various careers have surprised a lot of people. "I have been told, 'You can't be a director making serious films and a TV comedian at the same time. It just can't happen. Why do you continue to do both?' My reply was that I like all the different hats that I wear. I have done many

things in my life. I have seen movies, I have played baseball and so on. Those experiences remain a part of me and I don't think there's any harm in having a lot of different interests. I hate so-called movie maniacs. By that I mean the kind of person who has been obsessed with film and only film since childhood. They start out with an 8mm VCR and they progress to making movies for the cinema. That's bullshit! That makes me want to say, 'Come on, you've got a whole lot to learn about real life!' Our imagination involves everything we have seen or done in our lives. If you ask a group of children to draw an animal they have never seen, they usually end up with something which looks similar to elephants or giraffes or whatever. We extract parts of our experience and knowledge, then add our own tastes to get what we call imagination. To me, directors or actors who don't have a depth of life experience are in real trouble. They are limiting themselves and the way that they see the world."

Takeshi was asked to what he credited this way of thinking. "I had this terrible teacher in primary school," he replied. "He was 20 years old and had just graduated from a junior college. Now, when I see 20-year-olds, I can't believe that a kid that age was one of my teachers! He used to get so angry that he'd hit us. One day, five of us had to line up in front of him to be punished for breaking some windows in the school building. He went down the line, punching us. I was the last one he got to, so I had to wait for my turn. I remember thinking, 'Oh no, he's going to hit me. Oh shit, he's coming! I'm scared.' Then, all of a sudden, I seemed to step out of my own body. I felt like I was watching myself being hit. And when it happened, I thought, 'Oops, Takeshi got punched.' It did hurt, but just as I was wondering how painful it was going to be, the part of me that was watching myself started to laugh. I know people say that when you die you have an out-of-body experience. Maybe I felt something similar.

Whatever, the experience stuck with me. Even when I'm on stage doing stand-up comedy, watching the crowd getting hotter, there is always another me inside trying to stay cool. That's what I mean when I say it's important to be able to draw on all sorts of different experiences." So how does Takeshi switch between Beat Takeshi and Takeshi Kitano, the director? "To me, Beat Takeshi is almost like a puppet which is manipulated by Takeshi Kitano. Whenever something goes wrong, it's Beat Takeshi who gets the blame. Takeshi Kitano is just watching him from above, saying, 'Oh, that Beat Takeshi did it again! Oops, his hand fell off.' What I'm concerned about is what happens to Takeshi Kitano and that's not a problem because the only thing I really fear is death. Any other problems, such as poverty or being punched or getting arrested, can be dealt with by Beat Takeshi alone!

"Once, I barged into the offices of Kodansha (a Japanese publisher). People asked me how I managed to put up with all the hassle I got for that. But to me, it was not Takeshi Kitano who did that, but Beat Takeshi. It was as though Takeshi Kitano said, 'Hey Beat! Can you do something about this?' and Beat Takeshi responded. So I could say that it had nothing to do with the real Takeshi Kitano." Death, or at least the scent of death, has played a big part in Takeshi's films. "When I was a kid, I was so scared of dying. I wanted to have girlfriends, I wanted to be rich, I had so many dreams to fulfil. What I didn't want was to go through my whole life as just some punk born to poverty. I was terrified of dying without ever having achieved anything.

"But one day, I came to realise that I couldn't keep running away. I had to tackle death face to face. That made me conscious of death. I thought that the best way for me to challenge it was to accept that I was willing to die." There is a story about Dustin Hoffman. When he was young, he was burnt so badly that he almost died. As he lay in bed, he thought of the better, more meaningful life he would live when he recovered. But later he said, "Ultimately, my philosophy of life didn't change at all. I learned only one thing − that my accident

> **It's like pointing to a beautiful woman and saying 'Have you ever had a woman like that? I have.'"**

could have happened to anyone." Takeshi agreed, "I went through a similar thing. I also had a near fatal accident that I was kind of hoping would change my life. I don't remember much about it. I ended up in hospital and I had to have an operation. Afterwards, my boss told me about it. He said it happened when I was on my motorcycle. But I just did that puppet thing again. I thought, 'Oh shit, Beat Takeshi's done it again!'

"Little by little, I discovered how serious the accident had been. I thought, 'This will change my life, perhaps make me more creative.' I even thought that my brain structure might have been changed and that it might make me more artistic. It convinced me to start painting. But at the end of the day, nothing changed at all! So the only thing I got out of that accident was that I could say to people, 'Have you ever had a near-death experience? You just have no idea about death, do you?' It's like pointing to a beautiful woman and saying 'Have you ever had a woman like that? I have'."

The subject of women has a particular relevance to Takeshi's films. Often, they appear to be rather forgiving of men. They can be watching men doing something bad and they just say, 'Oh, men are so silly!' There aren't many scenes involving women, but yet the ones that do are always important. "I picture women as a sort of canvas," explains Takeshi. "I'm not saying men and women are so different. But women seem to me to be part of a much larger picture. It's as though they are the canvas, the mother earth, and men just happen to be doing something on it. I always feel that women are watching calmly, allowing men to carry on doing whatever it is they do. So it is difficult to think about me coming up with a story in which men and women are going fifty-fifty with each other. I'm thinking of basing my next film on a couple, but they certainly won't have a copybook marriage. The story may end in tears, but the idea is to depict a relationship which is not ordinary, but is still true to life.

"Men are definitely dependent on women. I'm no exception. I fling myself on my wife, or even on other women. Mostly, I want them to listen to my drivel. I feel like I'm looking for consolation when I go home at night. I'll say, 'I blew it again,' and my wife goes, 'No, you didn't. I know you.' When she says, 'You just be yourself, do whatever you want and don't worry about us,' it means so much to me. I know some people see me as a terrible guy who deserted his family, but that's not true. I do feel that I'm here thanks to my wife, and other women. I've never hustled other women, by the way, but I do have women who have always looked after me. They are good to have, despite the fuss other people may make about it.

"I sometimes wonder though if it makes me a grown-up mama's boy. What I mean by that is not that I'm dependent on my parents, but that I end up acting like a naughty child. I'll do something that I know I shouldn't, and as soon as I'm told off for it, I'll stop and shut up and shrink into myself like a little kid. For example, I might say to a woman, 'Oh, you ugly! Who do you think you are?' I know full well that I'll end up saying sorry

Sonatine

right after they tell me to get lost. I see the telling-off coming, but I still say what I shouldn't. Do you see what I mean? I'm not being nasty on purpose. I'll just do something on the spur of the moment, then go away once someone gives me an angry look. It's like poking a lion in the cage with a stick. If it roars at you, you run like hell, but of course, you know it can't hurt you because it's locked in a cage." Has Takeshi ever been in such a situation, certain he was safe, then discovered that the lion's cage was not locked after all? "No, not like that. But I wouldn't be that careless when dealing with women. I know how powerful they can be. It's like when I see bodhisattva. They can be fearsome and they can punish us. But I think you have to understand that if you want to be in a relationship with a woman. I sometimes see a man talking to a woman as though he's teaching her a lesson or something. I can't stand that because basically the man is just trying to prove something to himself. Anyway, the difference between that sort of guy and myself is that I know I'm not just getting what I want. I'm also putting myself in a potentially risky situation. There's always some element of risk involved in a relationship with a women and I have to admit that I rather enjoy those risks. I know that

ABOVE **Getting Any?** BELOW **Kids Return**

it might all go wrong and I'll end up getting bad-mouthed. But life would be boring if it had only ups and no downs.

"The same can be said about Takeshi Kitano films or about Beat Takeshi. Playing with a ready-made toy is not nearly as much fun as fooling around with one that you have to build yourself. The enjoyment is in trying to figure out how to get it to work." Also, if you start out with a finished product, the only difference you can make to it is to break it. "Exactly. How much fun would life be if we were all born perfect? The real fun in life is the fact that you go through it not knowing what's coming next. The new experiences we have, the things we see and feel that perhaps we didn't expect, those are the most important things." And so you feel much more positive or blessed if you live your life like that? "I think so.

"For instance, when I eat out, I don't have to go to a well-known restaurant. What makes me happy is when I happen to go into some restaurant I've never been to before and it turns out to be one of the best I've ever eaten at. I find that a lot here in Cannes. I can eat at expensive restaurants in posh hotels, but if I go into town, I can maybe find a small restaurant specialising in provincial cuisine, run by an old lady that no-one's ever heard of. Even if I'm the only customer, she'll still cook a whole range of dishes like mussels or whatever. Those dishes would be quite expensive if I was in Tokyo, but here they're comparatively cheap. You can even find wines and liqueurs at a surprisingly low price. Whenever I do that, I love it and I'm always really satisfied." That old lady in the restaurant, you know she'll still put 100% effort into making sure you're happy, even though you are her only customer. It must be her love of cuisine and her own pride in what she does. "Yes, and it's also a cultural thing too because, in this

particular instance, when I told her that I would like to come back the following day, she said that the restaurant would be closed. She takes every Sunday and Monday off, plus even when it's open, there are only ever a few customers who come, yet she can make a living like that. I think it shows that this country has class. You don't have to work too hard to have a good quality of life in a country which has real richness."

The Taiwanese director, Hou Hsiao-Hsien (who made *A City of Sadness*) was one of the faces spotted at the party after the official screening of *Kids Return*. Takeshi said to Hou, who has been dubbed the 'director of poetry' by the public: "I knew straight away that I shouldn't mess with you. I've heard that you used be really wild. I can tell that's true because I feel like the pair of us have a lot in common." After that, the two hit it off and had a great time hanging out together. While in Cannes, Takeshi also revealed another side of himself. Having recently resumed piano lessons, he had brought a keyboard with him to the festival on which to put in some practice. However, he discovered that the dexterity of his fingers was far from what he had hoped. "Oh you, you're useless!" he said of his own fingers. Takeshi Kitano, wild and yet sweet. These days, it's rare to find such a person of whom his fellow countrymen can be proud to call Japanese.

VENICE '97

'The Golden Lion goes to Hana-Bi''

by Yuki Sato

As Jane Campion announced the winner of the prestigious Venice Film Festival 1997 prize in front of the world's press, applause filled the room. For once, the gathering of journalists looked convinced. Usually, they greeted the winner with ruthless boos. One journalist from Hong Kong made his feelings clear: "I told you he'd win, didn't I?" A young Korean journalist said, "People in Korea should see Takeshi's films. I hope this award makes many more people aware of his talent." News of Takeshi's new-found fame in European countries such as England and France had got back to his fans in the Far East.

In Venice, the film director organised a brief press conference in his hotel suite, for Japanese journalists only. In the room was a stack of pot noodles, not what one would expect to find in an award-winning director's suite. "I knew I was getting favourable criticism this time," explained Takeshi. "That made me rather cautious and I tried not to read too much into it. In fact, this morning, a TV director told me that he had had a dream in which I won the Silver prize. I thought 'Oh shit!'. I also noticed that before the ceremony, people were sort of avoiding me as if they knew I hadn't won. It was as though they felt pity for me, like 'Oh, here comes poor Kitano'."

Takeshi's film *Hana-Bi* is a well-measured mix of tenderness and violence. It depicts the life of a retired cop who is willing to pay any price to help his ex-colleagues, but also has a cathartic side to him, shown through the relationship with his terminally ill wife. Takeshi joked that it was the best actor's award he had wanted to win. "I thought that would sell my name more widely and bring me bigger commercial success. Of course, at the end of the day, I'm sure that the Golden Lion is the one to win."

Only minutes after winning his award, Takeshi seemed to snap back into reality. He was in no mood to wallow in his success. He said, "I know that if I think of myself as an award-winning director, even for a fraction of a second, my next film would be a disaster. That's the biggest danger. Maybe I'll just celebrate by partying hard, and forget all about it. Then, just before I die, I'll think back on this as one of the highlights of my life. I can't get carried away with it if I want to keep on making good films. "What this award really means to me is that, as the kind of director who is labelled as minority or cult, I have made an inroad into the mainstream so that people who come after me will find it easier to do the same. That's what I mean when I say that I'm like a cancer in the body of the Japanese film industry. That's the answer I always give when foreign journalists ask me what I am. And I'm proud of it!"

When *Kids Return*, Takeshi's last film, was shown at the Cannes Film Festival, Japanese and European journalists interpreted the last line very differently. Did anything similar happen with *Hana-Bi* in Venice? "Yes, it did. You're talking about the line between the two main characters in *Kids Return* that goes 'We're not finished yet'. In Europe, it was perceived as 'It's all over',while it was seen as a positive message in Japan. It was an

> **A stack of snack noodles on a chest wasn't certainly the view I expected in the award winning director's suite**

interesting contrast. With that in mind, I thought that this film might be seen as totally insane. Think about it. The main character is an ex-cop. He cares for his crippled former partner and, at the same time, robs a bank for his ill wife and takes her on a trip that leads to their own demise. I was worried that critics might try to look at that character rationally and just think, 'This is sheer nonsense. Such a person cannot exist'. But I reckon that we Japanese would somehow see a virtue in such insanity, like Kamikaze to take an extreme example. I played this main character as a rebel to make a point of this vanishing virtue and to say, 'Here is just another way one can go through life'. I didn't expect people in Europe to buy the idea and I was ready to accept a lot of criticism for it.

"However, it turned out that they might have understood the message better than the Japanese. That was a nice surprise, but also kind of frightening. Frightening because it showed that the idea is universal? "I think it may reflect a time lag in terms of cultural understanding. Now, when people in Europe look at Japan, they are beginning to understand the soul that we Japanese treasured some decades ago, but have almost forgotten these days."

Another impressive aspect of *Hana-Bi* was the

way that Takeshi depicted the life of two characters, a married couple, who have no qualms about living on the edge of society. The wife, played by Kayoko Kishimoto, looks just like a little girl. "I think that had something to do with the comedian in me. It may be unusual for a director, but for me, it's only natural to try to come up with punch-lines and then try to get the best out of them. In *Hana-Bi*, the challenge for me was how I could make the biggest possible impact with the last line, spoken by the main character's wife. In fact, at one point during the shoot, I said to myself, 'What if this girl (the wife) knows everything her husband has done? That would be kind of scary and it would give much more depth to the film'. So I developed the story, which I think worked well."

And is the character truly insane? "Every time I hear women saying 'I want to be loved by a guy like him', I go, 'Are you really sure?' The guy is a classic nutcase in a comedy situation. We're supposed to laugh at him. In the film, someone says to him, 'Are you crazy or what? How dare you do such a thing!' Then in comes the punch line: 'By the way, what was it like? I've always wanted to do that'."

The conversation between Taiwanese director Hou Hsiao-Hsien and Takeshi at the after-screening party for *Kids Return* in

> **I shall be like, just before I die, remembering this as one of the events in my life**

Cannes revealed a lot about Takeshi's instincts. Finding himself seated next to Hou at a table, Kitano's opening comment was, "I bet you were a wild guy when you were young." A surprised Hou asked how he knew. Takeshi explained that he could tell from Hou's films. "I sense the same vibe in your work that I have in mine," he said. "It tells me that your motivation comes from all the crap you've gone through in the past."

One interesting discrepancy between the work of the two directors is that Hou likes to prominently feature dining scenes in his films, while Takeshi never does. Takeshi has even claimed that he feels uncomfortable shooting such scenes. "In Hou's films, there is always a clattery

dining scene which is well synchronised with the tone and the pace of the film itself. I admire the skill that it takes to do that, but I've never tried it myself. Perhaps the same can be said about me and the sea. I love the sea and there's always scenes shot by the seaside in my films. I'm obsessed with the colour of the sea, all those different shades of blue. I try to create my own kind of blue – I call it 'Kitano's Blue' – based on the colour of something like the thick water of the seas around Japan. It's odd

because I never have the desire to go into the sea. I mean, I do love the sea, but at the same time, something inside tells me to keep a distance from it. We all know our origin is in the sea and it feels to me as though Mother Nature is calling us home. But on the other hand, that's all in the past – we know we no longer belong there. There seems to be a fine line that we shouldn't cross."

So what do dining scenes mean to Takeshi? "To me, the dining scene is a very dirty subject to deal with. It seems inextricably linked with sex and excretion – and that's a little too much for me. That's why I only shoot scenes which take place either directly before or right after dining. I can't ever see me shooting a scene in which the characters are talking between mouthfuls of food. Hou does it well, but I couldn't. I think it has a lot to do with being Japanese. Things like dining and sex may be a part of our daily lives, but that doesn't mean we have to show them to other people. Traditionally in Japan, it was thought best to hide things like that. Everyone knew that the dirty side of life existed – you could see it in Japanese pillow books – but it was not a topic for open discussion. Even now in Japan, if a guy is looking for a sex, he'll approach it in a roundabout way. He'll take a girl to dinner in the hope that he'll get what he wants in the end. But the couple in *Hana-Bi* seem very far removed from that filthiness.

"It is said that nowadays men and women are in fifty–fifty relationships. I don't think things are that simple. Also, it depends on the type of relationship in question. It could be between a mother and son, or a father and daughter. In *Hana-Bi*, there isn't much conversation between the couple and that was intentional. That was maybe because of the comedian in me, preferring to concentrate on the punch line. Also, conversation would have required communication between the two. That communication could have led to physical contact and I didn't want that happening in my film. So I

took a more and more stoical direction and the conversation grew less and less. I was convinced that nothing physical was needed between the two, that smiles were enough to let the audience know what was going on."

Does Takeshi feel that too much emphasis is now placed on the physical side of relationships? "I'm not proud to admit this, but when I was starting to make a name for myself as a comedian, I used to treat women as just sex objects. I was like that until about the age of 35."

That's a young age to 'retire'? "Yeah, it's early. Although I didn't really 'retire' until I was 40. I'm not saying I stopped wanting to have sex, I just began to appreciate both physical and stoical relationships. The world has gone mad about sex. I didn't want to make the sort of film that has the audience counting the sex scenes. That's pointless! I'd rather offer something else instead."

Europeans are perhaps better equipped than the Japanese to understand the mentality behind

Getting Any?

Takeshi's films, and yet many seem to have a hard time digesting Beat Takeshi's sense of humour. In *Getting Any?* one restaurant scene shows a wall with framed portraits of a dynasty of Yakuza clan bosses:

at the start of the row there's a photo of the latest boss, followed by a heavily moustachoied boss from the early 20th century, then bosses depicted on famous Japanese ukiyoe prints by Sharaku, and finally squatting 'period' bosses on antique Japanese terra cotta figurines. In another scene a completely meaningless conversation in a foreign language is given Japanese subtitles – supposedly by Natsuko Toda, a leading cinema subtitle translator in Japan – which has nothing whatsoever to do with the actual conversation. European audiences find it hard to grasp such nonsensical humour. Takeshi, however, seems unconcerned about this. He even joked, "What I want to do is make a serious film like *Hana-Bi*, then also make a complete parody of it. Then I'd release the two together, to be watched one after the other."

Are Takeshi's films still labelled violent by some critics? "As far as *Hana-Bi* is concerned, I was told by many foreign journalists that I had managed to make violence co-exist with tenderness. They saw the violence in that film as coming from a completely different angle than it had in my previous films. They asked me if I had changed my attitude towards violence. But it wasn't like that. It was just that I needed something by which I could be recognised at that time and, to me, that was violence. That's my answer to that question. Once I was well-known, I could then take it on to the next level. I could experiment more and do whatever I wanted. That said, people told me that I was jumping the gun with *Getting Any?* But what I was trying to say to other directors was that they shouldn't be making films if they have no sense of humour. You don't have to use your sense of humour, but you do have to have one. But some people never seem to get that and I'm sick of them."

Takeshi has said that he doesn't like 'film maniacs', that is to say people to whom film is everything. "To make a film, you have to be aware of everything that's going on around you, of society as a whole. At least, that's the way I see it. So what can you do if you only have a tiny piece to start with? Put it this way, you only get a diamond by polishing a much bigger rock. It's essential to begin with a bigger picture. The challenge is how you refine that. Some people seem to skip that process and go straight for the end product. I don't think that's right."

As news of Takeshi's growing status abroad has spread back to Japan, he has been hailed as

something of a hero in his homeland. Does he now think of himself as a famous film-maker? "I'm just happy to be a big shot. You know why? Because I'm still a comedian at heart. Have you seen Francis F. Coppola out in public dressed only in his underpants? I can't wait to be able to do that sort of thing myself. If I was to compare my career to the swing of a pendulum, I would want it to be in full swing. As I become famous all over the world, people look at me with admiration and go, 'Wow, that's Kitano!' In the meantime, I'm always ready to pull some stunt to grab everyone's attention.

"Most people try not to put themselves in such a vulnerable situation, but I'd rather go for it if that's what it takes to swing the pendulum a little bit higher." Has Takeshi thought that way since he first began making films? And is Takeshi Kitano becoming bigger now that Beat Takeshi? "I must confess that when I started making films, I almost decided to call a halt to my comedy career. I remember that when I was making *Sonatine*, I was sure that my heart was in filmmaking, so I wanted to push myself in that direction. But then I took a step back to think about it. I was so into filmmaking that it was all I cared about. I was very narrow-minded. I realised that if I wanted to swing my pendulum high in one direction, it would have to be swung equally in the other direction. That was the only way to do it.

"That made me think about the other direction, in other words, my comedy as well as my filmmaking. I also think that my motorcycle accident may have been a blessing in disguise. It put me in a totally different

Takeshi with Joe Hisaishi (RIGHT) at the official screening in Venice

frame of mind. It made me feel good about doing comedy again. I'm very happy with the way things are going right now. I feel like the pendulum is in full swing and that's encouraging. When I start shooting a new film, it's as though the film itself gets a personality. I almost let it decide for itself what it's developing into. Of course I'm still officially the director, but I know better than to interfere in its natural direction. It would be a mistake to do so. I'd rather just say, 'Film, go in any direction you want!' "

Cheers with Masayuki Muri (LEFT) Joe Hisaishi (RIGHT)

HANA-BI

KITANO ART GALLERY

His aim in painting is very simple. As Takeshi said, "Why did I start painting? After the motorbike accident I did it as a kind of rehabilitation. I'd heard about people's hidden genius flourishing after a serious blow to the head. Before I began painting I half expected to get a flash of artistic inspiration." His first attempt was to copy Vincent van Gogh's Sunflowers, turned into a disaster, a million miles away from van Gogh's masterpiece. "That was the first time for me to draw seriously. It didn't bear the slightest resemblance to van Gogh's Sunflowers. So I painted a sunflower on a lion's head as a gag. They were perfectly matched. Then I got more and more ideas about painting." That was how he found that painting made him very peaceful and happy. In the aftermath of his motorbike accident he had a lot of spare time and really enjoyed it. Geijyutsu Shincho, a monthly Japanese art magazine, became interested in his paintings and started to introduce his works in their publication. Many people,

especially established painters and artists, were astounded to know that Takeshi had such a marvellous talent as an artist. But he didn't admit himself as a painter. "I didn't know how they found out about my paintings. Anyway they said they wanted to publish some of them in their magazine. They were very interested in my parody versions of masterpieces. "Takeshi didn't take their offer so seriously. He titled his pages in Geijyutsu Shincho, 'Takeshi's Lavatory Graffiti'. Gradually his involvement in painting grew deeper. Every month he tried new techniques, from using marker pens to pointillism. Finally he used his favourite 37 paintings in his film Hana-Bi. Originally he hadn't planned to use any of these paintings in the film. When he wrote the scene of a wheelchair-sticken Horibe, now a retired detective after being shot and paralyzed, he wanted his character to paint. "If he doesn't have a job, how will he spend his free time? Maybe he would paint like me. Of course he was a beginner, an amateur painter, so I decided to use my paintings as they were." In Hana-Bi, a pink and white clothed angel with blue wings (the picture on the left page) appears in the opening credits. All the bright colours come from poster colours, marker pens and pastels. Why an angel? "I envy angels, 'cause they are floating in the air. One of the human being's disadvantages is of always being drawn to the earth by gravity."

The White Snow is formed from hundreds of chinese characters for the word 'snow'. The red characters in the centre of the painting symbolise blood and mean 'suicide.
Takeshi said, "Blood is best reflected on white. White reflects very well under the light. So there is a spirit in this painting."
HANA-BI

Hana-Bi means 'fireworks' which bring happiness to a family on a summer's night
HANA-BI

OVERLEAF Six yakuza and a variety of tattoos and penises. "Our hidden culture is vanishing so I focused on its exposure"
HANA-BI

The Sunflower Lion was created after he failed to make a good copy of van Gogh's Sunflowers
HANA-BI

KIKUJIRO

KIKUJIRO

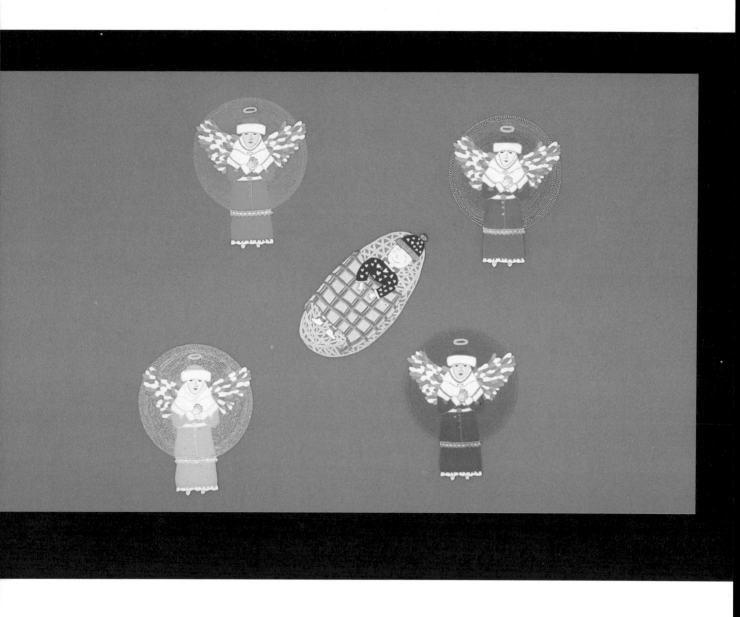

KIKUJIRO AND OVERLEAF

ビートたけし大先生の教室シリーズ
―ナンパについて―

今回のこの教室シリーズは、たけさんの大好き（？）な、ナンパについてで、あります。彼が日頃からよく言っているナンパの事を、鋭く聞いてみましたので、ニヤニヤしながら、読んで下さいませ!! ―この日のたけさんはまたまた、相変らずにねむそぉーな眼を、していらっしゃいました。

D.C―えっと今回は、ナンパについてです。
「ナンパについてね・・・うん。」
D.C―たけさんは、ラジオでよく女の子をナンパしたとか、言ってますけど、それは本当の事ですか？
「え―――。5割!! この間の大阪みたいに、悲惨な事件だった。（笑）」
D.C―どういう感じの女の子に、いいよるんですか？
「どういう感じもないんだよ、別に……（笑）」
D.C―年は、どれくらいの子ですか？
「もう……広く。」
D.C―女の子は、ちゃんと誘いにのりますか？
「うーんとね。今は、誘いにのるっっんじゃなくて、誘われちゃうんだよね。自らが、誘ったつもりはないけど、ついてきたりして、困っちゃう時が、あるんだよね……。」
D.C―誘う時は、どーいうふうに言って誘うんですか？
「どういうっっのもなーー……（笑）。うん。」
D.C―ズバリ！ナンパの目的は？（笑）
「ズバリ、ナンパの目的（笑）……ナンパの目的は、ナンパですよ、そりゃ（笑）」
D.C―場所は？どーいう所ですか？
「最近は、もうねぇ……飲み屋だね。」
D.C―いつも1人でナンパするんですか？
「いや」
D.C―友達と？
「だから、みんなが集まると、そういう状態になっちゃうんだよ。1人で、どこどこ行って、なんて絶体ないもん。1人で歩かないでしょ。んーん、たまに行くとこは、料理屋いって2階で、1人で飲んでるけど……みんなが集まるから、人のいる所へ行くだけであって。1人だけで、人のいる所へなんか、行ったことがない。だから、常に高田さんとか、片岡とかね。昨日は、さんまとか、竜助とか、たくさんいれば、それで仲間で、ディスコとか、行こうってことになるけど……1人でディスコなんて、とんでもない。」
D.C―ディスコってどこらへんの？

「うーん大阪のやつが、出てくるとやっぱり六本木に行くからサ。あのへん……。」
D.C―原宿でよく女の子を、ナンパしている男の子たちが、いるけど、そーいう事をどう思いますか？
「非常に、良い事だと思うね。うーん原宿で共に原宿ぶって上がって歩いてるのいるけどいい思い出になるんじゃないの（笑）」
D.C―自分も仲間に入りたいと思いますか？
「いや、思わない……（笑）俺は……」
D.C―あ！ナンパする時のヒケツなど
「うーんだから俺は、TVとか出てて、たけしつうのを知ってるから、ナンパできるだけであって、その普通の学生の子が、なにもなくて歩いてて言うつうのは、よっぽどの色男とか、よっぽどのスゴイ会話のうまい奴とかしかないんだと思うね。本当は、おいらぐらいにこう……もうだから僕らは、ナンパとは言えないんだよね。はっきり言えば……向うから、近づいて来ちゃう。こっちから声をかけて、どうだこうとは、ないからね。だからそのヒケツは、わからない。本当に、そういう事を、しているのだろうかと思うのね。」
D.C―じゃ、もしたけしさんが会社員とかだったら、ナンパをしていたでしょうね？
「絶体しないだろうね。したくて……したくてしょーがないと思うだろうけど。そんな勇気は、全々ない。それにモテやしないだろうし……初めから結果わかってるし、誰も相手にしないつう。俺、漫才師だから、なんか相手にしてくれるんじゃない。お笑いの世界に、いるから。俺がちゃんとした会社で働いていればさ、背広着てるわけだからサ、頭分けたりしてサ！（笑）そんなもの、女の子相手にするわけないじゃない。君たちにも『おじさん、何を言ってるんですか？』だよ。『イエズス会、入りなさい』って言われるよ。」

以上で、おわかりいただけましたように、ラジオで強気になってあーだ、こーだと言っていらっしゃるたけさんの内面は、非常に……なのであります。また、たけしさんの隠れた内面を、見ることができて、うれしく思っています。

P.S. でも、たけさんの七、三の頭、見たいよーな、見たくないよーな。あ！ひょうきん族に出ましたか？あーそうですか……ふぅーん。

A COMEDIAN STAR IS BORN

"Avant-Garde and Outrageous"

by Tomohiro Machiyama

I have been a huge Beat Takeshi fan since the start of his career. I was at junior high school then. I used to listen to all of his midnight radio programmes. He did those for a decade, but I only ever missed a few. However, I have met him just once in person. It was six years ago, when I was working as an editor of a magazine. A colleague of mine was interviewing him and I tagged along. I remember Takeshi saying, "Owarai(Comic Performance) is like a never ending move." That was a theory of his which he brought up a lot. He would say things like, "If I talk badly about the Yakuza and they get angry and come after me, I'll just apologise and run off. I'll say sorry and run. Or maybe 'Fuck!', then run." He'd also say, "Comic performers shouldn't take responsibility for what they have said and done." When you look closely at Takeshi's life, you find that it does reflect his theory, quite clearly in fact. It's just one continuous sequence of running away from everything, of never getting caught. The very first time he put that theory into practice was when he ran away from home.

When Takeshi was working as an apprentice at France Theatre in Asakusa, shortly after he had dropped out of university, dreaming of becoming a comedian, Kiyoshi Kaneko (aka Jiro) suggested that

...from a strip joint to comedy theatres and then to larger halls

the pair should do a manzai (stand up comedy) together. That was what eventually led to the formation of the The Two Beats manzai duo. Their stage names were Beat Takeshi and Beat Kiyoshi. They started out in strip joints and comedy theatres, then as they got more famous, moved on to larger halls. In 1976, they appeared on television for the first time and instantly became a social phenomenon. The reason was that the manzai that Takeshi spewed out was so different to the conventional manzai. His was much more risqué.

The subjects of Takeshi's manzai were a variety of socially vulnerable people such as the elderly, children, the disabled, the poor, the ugly, the stupid, even women. He cracked one gag after another about them. There is a famous quote from his Two Beats days which goes, "Make sure to firmly wring your parents' necks before you go to bed." It was a parody of a safety slogan by the fire brigade which originally went, "Make sure to firmly turn off the gas before you go to bed." In Japan at that time, the average life expectancy had grown and elderly people had begun to dominate the population. Domestic problems arose in every household from having to take care of elderly parents who might be bedridden or approaching senility. And so the tension between wives and their parents-in-law also grew. There were actual cases where parents were strangled by their son and his wife because young couples were so exhausted from endless caring. There was one instance where

A page from The Two Beats fanzine

a wife stabbed her mother-in-law. That explains why the television centre which aired the show was bombarded with phone calls from viewers offended by what they saw as tasteless gags. The complaints persuaded the station to ban Takeshi from doing certain jokes and to edit the footage and take out any offensive dialogue.

While the rest of society was enraged by the duo, the younger generation – mostly in their early twenties or younger – adored Takeshi's anti-social, anti-humanitarian jokes, which is why The Two Beats became so popular. Consequently, some critics gave the show glowing views. They said things like, 'The Two Beats possess a high level of irony which discloses the true feeling of society, namely that the elderly are a burden'. Some even called Takeshi Japan's answer to Lenny Bruce.

The best-known Two Beats joke is a parody of a public transport safety slogan which goes, "Cross when the traffic lights are at red, like everyone else and you will be safe." Initially, that was attacked for encouraging children to break road safety rules. Eventually, however, people came to see it as poignant criticism of the collective psychology particular to the Japanese – i.e. 'If you can't beat 'em, join 'em'. But was sharp-tongued social criticism really what Takeshi was aiming for? I think not. Lenny Bruce was another comedian who made a point of using racially discriminating words such as 'nigger', which were taboo in his time. His act was described as focusing the spotlight on discrimination which is hidden from public media and the surface of society, but which actually exists in the very depths of it'. But was that right? When they were not dealing with discrimination, both Lenny and Takeshi joked about death and illness. The reason was that these subjects were not

The Two Beats Fanzine

considered funny. Likewise, both men repeatedly used words like, 'dick', 'cunt', 'shit' and 'puke'. They chose these because they were words that most people thought should not be uttered in public, let alone broadcast to the nation. It's like being a child, when the more your parents tell you not to say certain words, the more you're tempted to shout them out loud. It's the same sort of childish urge that makes Takeshi want to say things he's not supposed to.

There was one sketch that Takeshi would persistently repeat which demonstrated the depth of his childishness. In it, he would call out, "Comaneci!", then make movements with his hands outlining a V-shape around his crotch. He first came up with this gag when he was talking about how erotic Nadia Comaneci, the Romanian Olympic gymnast, looked in her groin hugging leotard. Takeshi took up a half squatting pose and used his hands to portray this image, while at the same time shouting, "Comaneci!". This in itself was not at all funny, but for some reason, Takeshi seemed to like it so much that he took to doing it at every opportunity. Soon, his audience joined in with the joke, but it was partly because they were appalled with Takeshi for doing, as one critic said, "Something so ludicrous for someone his age (Takeshi was already in his thirties)." But that was precisely what Takeshi was aiming for. The intention of the Comaneci gag was to stop the public from seeing him as an arrogant man who used his intelligence to spray poison-tongued sarcasm. When he told the joke, Takeshi wasn't a sarcastic guy with brains, he was one of those lads in the classroom who is always being cheeky to the teachers and getting told off. Like Bart Simpson! That's why it was kids at kindergarten or at primary school who enjoyed the joke the most. They may not have understood Takeshi's manzai, but they got the Comaneci gag. They proved it by placing their hands on their groins and being told off by their parents and teachers.

Takeshi escaped from the convention of graduating from university to become what he called "a member of society". He turned his back on life as a 'sensible adult' and chose instead to keep on acting like a child. When he became a comedian, he was already in his thirties, but referred to himself as "Takechan", which is what a mother might call her child. He called his own mother "okaachan"(ma). Often, he would bring his mother's stories into his act, then repeat words like 'dick' and 'shit'. That showed that he was not a grown-up, but a big kid. His theory that "owarai is like a never ending move" can be interpreted as 'Keep being a cheeky, naughty child who plays pranks, then runs off'.

I once wrote that, "Takeshi's manzai is an expression of his childish urge to explode". In that sense, I think Takeshi's attitude was similar to the spirit of rock'n'roll – i.e. bollocks to adult common sense and sound judgment.

Until The Two Beats came along, the elderly appreciated manzai. That changed when The Two Beats sent scores of junior high and high school students (including myself) into a frenzy. Soon, other so-called 'New Wave' manzai duos sprung up and the 'manzai boom' was born. To young audiences, manzai was the equivalent of rock bands.

Technically-speaking, however, The Two Beats' manzai was not proper manzai. Takeshi had never been a big manzai fan, nor had he studied it or become an apprentice to a particular master. His manzai totally ignored the traditional roles of boke (fall guy) and tsukkomi (joke teller). In the conventional form of manzai, the tsukkomi introduces the subject. Then the boke follows with an obtuse answer, to which the tsukkomi responds with a phrase like 'Don't be stupid' and whacks the boke. Takeshi's manzai was different. It was almost a monologue. He would gibber on, speaking in speedy rhythms of speech reminiscent of his native Tokyo. He'd say things like, "How about a sex doll that awards scores at the end? After you've used it,

The Comaneci! pose

it gives you technical points and artistic points". The problem was that Kiyoshi was too slow to come up with a snappy response. Kiyoshi was from Tohoku, in the north of Japan, where the climate is more severe than in Tokyo. People from Tohoku tend to mumble their words, as they are used to opening their mouths as little as possible because of the cold. When Takeshi made one of his off-the-cuff comments, all Kiyoshi could manage to reply was, "What are you talking about?". There was never any decent conversation between them.

The manzai boom grew to the extent that a festival was organised at the Nippon Budokan, an indoor stadium where the likes of The Beatles and Deep Purple once played. By the time the eighties arrived, Takeshi had stopped making appearances as The Two Beats and started to perform solo. Consequently, he established himself away from the manzai boom, as well as from The Two Beats.

In 1981, Takeshi began hosting a radio show once a week. *All Night Nippon* was aired every night, starting at 1a.m., and the majority of its listeners were junior high or high school students, who were supposedly studying in their bedrooms. The show was based on postcards sent in from listeners, who had been given a topic to write about the previous week. The host would then read out the postcards and make comments on them. Takeshi's topics included, "How to recognise a person who pretends to be an ultra-trendy city slicker, but really comes from the countryside" and, "How to spot someone who is now middle-class, but grew up poor". One of his favourite themes was discrimination. His most popular, however, was "How to wank – the New Way." That one drove his adolescent audience wild. They used their imaginations to the full to come up with responses. One went, "First, go to a farm where they have lots of dairy cows. Take out the cow costume that you brought with you, then wear it with your dick sticking out of the nipple part. An innocent milkmaid, a look-a-like of Heidi of the Alps, heroine of the book by Joanna Spyri, will come along and give you a hand-job, thinking that she is just milking a cow." Others were even more outrageous. For example, "If you ever get the chance to go on a school trip to Kyoto or Nara and stay the night at a temple, try beating the mokugyo (a wooden block used for praying in Buddhist temples) in the middle of the night, when all the priests are sound asleep. Without waking up, a priest who is dedicated to his beliefs will start to mouth the lines of the scriptures. Then you appear on the scene – or rather your dick does. Into the priest's mouth you go, off to jerk heaven!" Or, "If you're masochistic, go to a studio where they are shooting the new series of Godzilla

> **"We used to get some firecrackers or 2Bs (similar to cherry bombs) and then stick them up frogs' arses and blow them up"**

movies and hide under the floorboards of one of the miniature sets. Then stick your dick through a hole in the floor. When filming starts, Godzilla and Radon will mistake it for Mothra and begin biting and punching it. They may even breath fire on it."

Another part of Takeshi's show was called 'Adachi-warders welcome'. It was based on his own experience as a child growing up in Adachi-ward, east Tokyo. Takeshi would tell stories from his childhood and asked the listeners to send in their own childhood tales. One went, "There were a lot of craftsmen in downtown Tokyo and most of them had tattoos. I don't know whether they couldn't tolerate the pain or they didn't have enough money, but several just had the outlines done and the rest wasn't coloured in. Kids had no idea how scary these guys could be, so they would go up to them in public baths, point at their tattoos and say, 'You've got pictures on your back!' They usually ended up getting a good slap." Another was, "When we went to a fair, there were stalls where you could shoot targets or throw rings. The top prize would be something like an expensive camera. The bullets were made out of cork, but even if you hit the target, it was rigged so that it would never topple over." Or, "We used to get firecrackers or 2Bs (like cherry bombs), then stick them up frogs' arses and blow them up." Thus, Takeshi shared his childhood memories with his listeners. He referred to his young audience as 'omaera' (you lot), which was how a gang leader would address his followers. In doing so, he became closer to his listeners, who looked on him as their boss or an older brother living next door.

Every week, at the start of his show, Takeshi would disclose personal secrets about himself. He even talked freely of his extra-marital affairs and revealed embarrassing stories about people in his immediate family, including his wife and his parents. Once, he said, "The other day, when my wife was doing the laundry, she turned to me and said, 'You've been flirting again, haven't you?' I asked what made her say that and she replied, 'I know you took your underpants off somewhere. You wore them inside out and got shit on the outside of them'." When Takeshi talked about his 'soapland' girl (a bath house call girl), whom he visited regularly, he used her real name and the girl was swamped by fans who wanted to become 'soap' brothers with Takeshi. The poor girl disappeared shortly afterwards, claiming that her body couldn't keep up with the high demand.

Often, Takeshi revealed other people's embarrassing secrets on *All Night Nippon* without their consent. He talked about a fellow comedians' womanising. He also claimed that some handsome celebrities and sportsmen seen posing on TV couldn't actually read a simple chinese character which even a primary school student could understand and said that, behind the scenes, many of them were disliked by their peers, although such things were traditionally kept under wraps. Takeshi somehow managed to gibber on about them without getting into trouble. He got away with it because his revelations had the nature of an innocent primary school kid who might boast in public that 'My dad wears a wig!'

After establishing himself as 'the big brother' of *All Night Nippon*'s adolescent audience, Takeshi turned his attention to TV, appearing in a show called *Oretachi Hyokinzoku* (We Are Jokers) from the spring of '81. Launched as a Japanese version of *Saturday Night Live*, *Oretachi Hyokinzoku* centred on short comedy sketches. With that programme, Takeshi captured the hearts of primary school children. In it, he played a superhero called Takechanman. Each week, his character fought a villain known as Black Devil, played by fellow comedian Sanma Akashiya. The pair indulged in childish pranks such as competing to see who would be the first fall off the top of log bridges and slippery slopes (all props made in the studio). The loser fell into a pool of mud or flour – a hilarious sight. In this programme Takeshi made a point of excluding any manzai and of avoiding the type of talk that he used in his radio shows, instead concentrating solely on childish games and ideas. Little kids loved it and soon Takechanman became as popular as the Super Mario Brothers.

However, Takeshi is not the type of person to sit back and bask in public adulation. The more accepted he became, the more uncomfortable he felt. Years before, when he was an up-and-coming comedian, he often attacked comedians who had

been radical and controversial in their youth, but had turned into inoffensive, household stars. He hated that they had abandoned the very asset that had brought them fame. "Comedians are supposed to make people laugh by doing things they're not allowed to do," he would say. "Once they start talking about family values and humanity, they're not comedians anymore." Such sell-out comedians were not exclusive to Japan. They could be also found in America – Bill Cosby was a perfect example. However, by this time, even Takeshi – who had always been seen as the epitome of anti-social behaviour – had started to develop a 'nice guy' persona with the public. In '82, as a way of rebelling against this impression if him, he repeatedly flashed his genitals on live TV. It was a typical Takeshi stunt. He was 'the man who was never caught out'.

At the same time, Takeshi proved himself to be a serious actor by appearing in the film *Merry Christmas, Mr. Lawrence*. The story was set in World War II and Takeshi played the part of humane Sergeant Gengo Hara. He made audiences around the world cry at the final scene, in which he awkwardly mutters his very first English words, 'Merry Christmas, Mr. Lawrence'. With his next film role, he shattered his 'good guy' image, playing the part of Kiyoshi Okubo, the most despicable serial rapist murderer in Japanese history.

Meanwhile, Takeshi continued to make his regular appearances on midnight radio. Fans who regarded him as a big brother took to hanging around the radio station where he worked and were taken on as his apprentices. They called themselves Gundan (Takeshi's Army) and referred to their idol as 'Tono' (My Lord), the name samurai gave to their masters. Takeshi planned several programmes for his 'Army', the first of which he called *Ganbaruman*. Army members were given atrocious dares, such as competing to see who could stay the longest in a boiling hot bath or buried stark naked up to their necks in snow. They were also challenged to fight lions and cobras, as well as professional boxers, whose punches could knock them out. One accepted a dare to become an apprentice to a stuntman and drive headlong into an explosion. The public was outraged at

Takeshi, who would just sit and watch his followers endure such horrors. They claimed that he was 'like the Emperor Nero, forcing his slaves to fight in the Colosseum'. They asked, 'What if someone dies?' To this, Takeshi replied tongue-in-cheek, "They say they'll do anything for me, so I'm testing them to see if they're telling the truth." Then he stuck his tongue out.

Fuun! Takeshi jou (Hero Takeshi Castle) was a programme which took the idea of *Ganbaruman* one step further. In it, members of both Takeshi's army and his audience were invited to complete a series of obstacle courses, which led eventually to Takeshi Castle. The entertainment was purely physical and visual. Contestants had to do things like jump across squares of polystyrene floating on a cold lake, avoiding chunks of wood which were dropped on them from above. It was like a real life Super Mario Brothers game, which became hugely popular and was distributed to many overseas countries.

Ultra Owarai Quiz was a combination of the two shows mentioned above. Along with the Gundan, one-hit wonders, unpopular comedians and actors (all craving for a break into TV) gathered in a TV station car park to take part in a game which involved grabbing hold of a ball with 'Atari' (You win) written on it. Any contestant who failed at this stage was sent home on the spot, without receiving any fee. Takeshi laughed his head off watching these poor 'celebrities' humiliate themselves. The ones who got through the first stage then had to get on a bus for a Magical Mystery Tour. They had to play games which involved things like answering questions while standing on top of a tall tower. If they gave a wrong answer, they were pushed off the tower, their feet tied to a rope like a bungee jump. Sometimes, they had to walk over ground with hidden landmines which would suddenly explode. *Sonatine*, the film directed by Takeshi in '93, was an extension of these bully-style shows. You can see it most clearly in the scene where Takeshi sets off fireworks aimed directly at his 'young brothers'.

While critics complained that his shows were a bad influence because they encouraged bullying, Takehi began writing novels. Both *Kids Return* and *Asakusa Kid* were about his own childhood in

Takeshi in the final and emotional scene from Merry Chrfistmas, Mr Lawrence

downtown Tokyo, while *Takeshi-kun, Hai!* – a children's book which he also illustrated – was a nostalgic account of his early years. All three were highly acclaimed and *Takeshi-kun, Hai!*, a bestseller, was even turned into a daily soap on national television. Once again, Takeshi was disturbed by his success as people began to suspect that not only was he far cleverer than he made out, but that he was also a kind, gentle person at heart.

Consequently, Takeshi went back on the rampage. In 1986, he broke into the editor's office of weekly photo journal *Friday* and got arrested. The public was appalled by his behaviour. Takeshi attacked the journal because it published a picture of his lover. Questioned about the incident, he said, "I have talked openly about my own womanising because it is part of my life. But my lover is not a public figure. Her privacy should not be invaded."

Takeshi had decided to raid the office while out drinking with members of his Army. He realised that it was the anniversary of the raid of Chuushingura (when Kuranosuke Oishi led 47 ronin in an attack on the Kira mansion in revenge for his master). Takeshi's intention was to parody the historical incident. He and the Army broke into the office, spraying the place with a fire extinguisher, which just happened to be handy. Significantly, spraying a fire extinguisher is common place in Japanese slapstick comedy, much like pie throwing. However, the staff at the *Friday* office did not see the funny side of it, and Takeshi and his Army were arrested on charges of intrusion and assault.

Some people criticised Takeshi for trying to dismiss the incident as a joke, but most of the general public stood up for him. They supported him not because he was famous or talented, but because he would not take a conventional, 'adult' attitude towards the paparazzi. Instead, he resorted to childish tactics, which were consistent with his character. That year, while the incident was still fresh in people's minds, Takeshi was ranked in the Top Five of an annual national survey of 'Most Likeable Celebrities'.

When I first heard about Howard Stern, a Shock Jock in New York, I was surprised at how similar he and Takeshi were. Although Stern is

Vioent Cop

190cm tall and Takeshi a little short of 170cm, both achieved cult popularity by using vulgar, radical language on radio. Both have also published best-selling autobiographies. Fartman, the alter ego of Howard Stern, is identical to Takechanman. Stern directed his own movie *Private Parts*, and Takeshi *Violent Cop*. The similarities end here, however, because while *Private Parts* was a heart-warming comedy which gave the public the impression that Stern might actually be a 'nice guy', *Violent Cop* was a cold-blooded, very violent piece of work. Takeshi may well have made such a movie to turn the general public off holding him in high esteem.

The violence in *Violent Cop* was unlike anything most movie-goers had ever seen. In the film, the violence occurs suddenly, when the audience is least expecting it. In commercial films, violent scenes tend to be preceded by certain camera angles and dramatic music. In Takeshi's work, shots are fired out of the blue and death can occur at any time. No matter how disturbing the action, the images are calmly shot, which somehow makes the scene seem even more shocking. Takeshi's style of unassuming violence is similar to the scene in Martin Scorsese's *Goodfellas* (1990) where Joe Pesci suddenly fires his gun in the middle of a poker game, or the scene in Quentin Tarantino's *Reservoir Dogs* (1991) when Chris Penn shoots the shackled cop. In another Tarantino movie, *Pulp Fiction*, the same type of direction is employed when Samuel L. Jackson shoots a young man making excuses for stealing his boss' money. Takeshi, however, began using the method before either of them.

In my opinion, the bluntness of the violent scenes in Takeshi's films are influenced by Jean-Luc Godard. For example, in *Vivre Sa Vie* (*It's My Life*) (1962), the heroine, Anna Karina, is shot mercilessly in the final scene. The off-beat gun raid in Godard's *Alphaville* was also an influence on Takeshi. He is said to have seen French New Wave films in art cinemas in the five years after he dropped out of university and was living a bohemian lifestyle. Indeed, Takeshi once wrote in the magazine Weekly Post, "You cannot understand my movies unless you are familiar with the work of Godard". Furthermore, the working title of his film *Sonatine* (1993) was Okinawa Pierrot, a play on Godard's film title *Pierrot Le Fou* (1965), and the story was adapted to the southern Japanese islands of Okinawa. Godard's attempt to deconstruct the system of film-making undoubtedly appealed to Takeshi, whose motto was "Keep on running, never get caught out" and who went out of his way to reject common sense and conventional ideas.

It is important to add that the violence in Takeshi's films is invariably accompanied by a wicked sense of humour. In *Violent Cop*, cinema audiences laughed after seeing an emotionless Takeshi blast his guns. Such violence combined with humour can also be seen in the killing scenes of Scorsese films starring Joe Pesci or in Tarantino films with Samuel L. Jackson. The fact that both Pesci and Jackson are excellent live comedians is another link to Takeshi. In short, the violence in Takeshi's movies can be viewed as simply an extension of his comedies.

For *Violent Cop*, Takeshi was highly-acclaimed as a director and won many prizes. He turned up to the Japanese Academy Awards wearing a Geisha outfit, which took away from the seriousness of the occasion. The more he became acknowledged as a writer and director, the more he appeared on television in fancy dress – often as a woman, a day labourer or a gorilla. It was as if to say, 'I'm not the grand person you think I am'.

In 1994, Takeshi was involved in an accident while riding his motorbike. The crash left his face damaged – one side of it remains paralysed to this day. The previous year, Takeshi had directed *Sonatine*, in which a middle-aged yakuza commits suicide after suffering existentialist agony. Takeshi himself had often spoken of his suicidal tendencies, so journalists quickly jumped to the conclusion that the incident was an attempt by Takeshi to take his own life. He did not deny the rumours. He simply said, "That incident was not suicide, but I do think a lot about dying these days." Why did Takeshi make such references to death? Perhaps because the public has got used to his outrageous antics and now takes whatever he does for granted. He can use as many controversial words as he likes, expose his genitals on TV, be convicted of violence or make blood-thirsty films, but the public can no longer be shocked by him. As a man who has to 'keep on running', the only means of escape left for Takeshi could be death.

The film that he was making at the time of his accident was his first ever slapstick comedy, Getting Any? It was eventually released in 1995 after Takeshi had been discharged from hospital. It starred Dankan – a member of the Takeshi Army – as a dull man who had never gone out with a woman. He tries everything under the sun to find someone to have sex with. The film was full of jokes about penises and shit, very vulgar and childish from beginning to end. Takeshi directed it under his stage name as a comedian, 'Beat Takeshi', no doubt to escape his reputation as Takeshi Kitano, the gifted director. I wonder what foreign critics, who had praised his previous films, thought of Getting Any? It may have been a vulgar movie, but this was the real Takeshi, the one that the Japanese knew and loved, both from television and from the radio.

Iesu No Hakobune won the Artistic Work award from the Agency for Cultural Affairs in Japan

TAKESHI: A GENIUS ACTOR

by Casio Abe

Beat Takeshi's career as an actor is grounded in his earlier success as a comedian. The style he favoured is known in Japan as manzai – stand-up comedy in which a pair of comedians work together as a double act. Having dropped out of a science & engineering course at university, he worked for a while as a barman, and doing other casual work. Eventually, however, he made his way to Asakusa, the mecca of traditional comedy in Japan in the early part of this century (although by the 1970's it was pretty run-down) where he formed a duo called 'The Two Beats' with fellow comedian Beat Kiyoshi. In those days, manzai comedy was not generally held in high regard, and they had to work on their act in strip clubs during breaks between performances, playing to audiences of drunks. But even at this stage, it was obvious that Takeshi had the makings of a star. The undisguised anger of his tone, directed at the shortcomings of society in the manner of Lenny Bruce, was too much for the customers, and the routines frequently fell flat – mainly because the audience simply could not keep up. What he was doing had no precedent in Japan, so it is hardly surprising that few people really appreciated his skill. But those who did understand were in no doubt about his genius.

Takeshi the comic bore the scars of his early days in the wilderness. That's why although there was always part of him that seemed to be voicing the anger of the underdog, there was also a sense in which this was defused by his inherent shyness and a tendency to sheer silliness. Whilst finding fault with all manner of things around him in the world, he would let himself get carried away in the act of speaking – and his face at such moments had this dazzlingly material quality to it. In fact, on the subject of 'material', there was always something about his stage presence that seemed more like a thing than a person. He also had this peculiar tic-like habit of jerking his head to one side. So

however harsh his words might seem to be, there was always a childlike quality to him that somehow reassured his audience. It was this quality, his accessibility, which eventually led to his becoming the most successful comedian in the history of Japanese television. He was lucky, too, that as one of the key figures in Japan's sudden manzai boom at the end of the 1970's, he was well placed for maximum exposure. The time was coming when he would have a place in the hearts of the whole nation.

Merry Christmas, Mr. Lawrence

Appearances in TV dramas and films only boosted his popularity, and he began to get more and more requests to appear as an 'actor', although those that wanted him for his name value were mainly interested in just having him show off his comic skills in front of the camera. The first person to understand and fully exploit what I have termed the 'material' quality of his character was the director of *Merry Christmas, Mr Lawrence*, Nagisa Oshima. Another fruitful opportunity came soon after this film. This was with a team from TBS, one of the major Japanese TV networks, headed by the producer Yasuo Yagi and the director Yamaizumi.

The first television drama to feature this material quality of Takeshi's character was *Okubo Kiyoshi no Hanzai* (The Crime of Kiyoshi Okubo) (1983). This was based on the true story of a man living in a country area far from Tokyo, who went round posing as an avant-garde artist. He used to sweet-talk young girls into his car, and then drive them off to deserted mountain areas where he raped and strangled them before burying them in shallow graves. These were horrific sexual crimes which shocked the whole nation, and the drama, in which Takeshi played the lead character, was impressive for the sheer range of his performance – Okubo's

lifestyle, criminal behaviour, and his behaviour during questioning being graphically linked through a series of complex flashbacks. Takeshi was meticulous in his portrayal of Okubo's childishness, his self-righteous attitude, his selfishness and insecurity, and in the violence of his crimes. This extraordinary story was also made into a film, starring Takuzo Kawatani, but Takeshi's bravura performance, with his ability to always keep a step ahead of the audience, outclassed even a man like Kawatani, so renowned for his acting ability. Takeshi wore the same clothes as Okubo was known to have worn, but he did not look anything like him. Despite this he was able to faithfully emulate the strangely material quality that people felt around Okubo.

How could he gain such a deep insight into

Okubo Kiyoshi no Hanzai

character of such a bizarre criminal? The key to this lies in his past. I have already mentioned, by way of example, that he worked as a barman. One of his colleagues at that time was a man called Norio Nagayama. They worked on different shifts, and so only saw each other at the changeover, and never actually worked together. But towards the end of the sixties, Nagayama got hold of a rifle and committed a series of murders, plunging the country into a state of terror. So the young Takeshi actually lived and worked in an environment that threw up a man like Nagayama.

Takeshi's face and body type are typically Japanese. Then there is the rapidity with which he switches from inscrutability to laughter, the slightly bandy legs, the powerful physique. We can perhaps understand the materiality of his presence as the sum of all these factors. They are all elements that can be put to the service of comedy, but at the same time are effective in portraying gangsters and criminals – types often seen as having a more material quality than ordinary people. Of course, his superb acting skills only reinforce this quality. As is clear from the films he directs himself, he never allows either himself or his fellow actors to appear to be acting. It is  enough for the actors to have a presence on screen – if they succeed in being real, then the film works. Takeshi learnt this the hard way in the school of manzai. For a comedian, contrivance is death: an off-hand, forceful manner wins laughs. Having tested the truth of this himself, he has become a pre-eminent exponent of the physical.

That's why he was able to give such outstanding performances in TV drama under the auspices of Yagi and Yamaizumi. His next role, in *Iesu No Hakobune* (The Ark of Jesus) (1985) saw him playing a man named Jesus Sengoku (to protect the man in question, he was given a name that was slightly different to the actual person the drama was based on). Sengoku had formed his own Bible study group, to whom a number of young women were

drawn. It was a self-sufficient and happy community, in which the girls abandoned their own families in order to form what they hoped would be a 'true' family living communally with Sengoku. But their parents did not see it that way, and protested that Sengoku had kidnapped their daughters – the whole affair eventually developing into a scandal that was taken up by the press. In the midst of all this, the film portrayed Sengoku's peripatetic religious community travelling around Japan, and illustrated the development of his personality using flashback techniques. But there was none of the violence that had been so shocking in his previous role. I have to confess that at the time I felt that, whilst there was a validity to the social issues being raised, it was rather lacking in edge for a drama featuring Takeshi in the lead role. But having recently seen it again, I've changed my mind. Through the character of Sengoku, Takeshi is brusquely expressing, somewhat ahead of himself, the same sadness present in the silences of the main character of *Hana-Bi*. There is an interesting tension, too, generated by the interplay with Kei Sato, one of Oshima's leading actors.

His next appearance in this series was in *Kim No Senso* (Kim's War) (1991), directed this time by Masaaki Odagiri. This dealt with a crime committed by Kim Hui Ro, a Japanese of Korean descent, when he was in his late sixties. Since childhood, Kim had been the subject of severe racial discrimination in Japan, and had had enough of it. He shot dead a gangster who had come to collect on an outstanding loan, and took refuge in a hotel, taking the guests hostage. His next move was completely unexpected. He invited a number of television and print journalists into the hotel, so that he could explain to the whole nation why he had been driven to commit this crime. By complaining openly about discrimination against Koreans, an issue that had consistently been brushed under the carpet in post-war Japan, he forced it into the public eye and created some vociferous support, especially from amongst the ranks of the Japanese New Left.

How did Takeshi play the character of this legendary criminal? In the same way, of course. Whilst giving a remarkably convincing portrayal of the behaviour of a person who has had resigned himself to life at the bottom of society, he masterfully evoked both the pathos of a man who has been denied both his nationalities – not able, even to speak his native (Korean) language – and the unique courage of someone driven to commit a rational crime which bordered on the altruistic. (There is a sense in which the moment that Kim is feted by the media overlaps with the image of Beat Takeshi, equally the media's darling). Also worthy of special mention is Kirin Kiki, who plays Kim's mother. She gives eloquent expression to the rightful pride of the Korean people, further enhancing the moral tone of the tragedy. In the final scene, Kim meets up with the Korean woman who has become his fiancee after an exchange of letters. The sight of Takeshi trying to communicate with her in the broken Korean he has learnt in jail is, of course, strongly reminiscent of the last scene of *Merry Christmas, Mr Lawrence*.

Takeshi also starred in a drama which was part of a series about people who have chosen to submit to the discipline of religious belief, in the same way as in *Iesu No Hakobune*. *Settoku* (Persuasion) (1993); with Yamaizumi back in the director's seat, is also the dramatisation of a real story. Jehovah's Witnesses are forbidden to receive blood transfusions on religious grounds. This film deals with the tragic story of a man who was, in effect, an accessory to his child's death from injuries received in a car accident by refusing to consent to the operation that would have saved his life. This pathetic foot soldier labouring in the front line of Japan's rapid post-war economic boom has found his only comfort and sense of purpose in religion – and so the question of consenting to a

Although there is little facial or bodily resemblance between Takeshi and this man, the chillingly 'material' quality is identical

blood transfusion for his son threatens to undermine his whole existence. The film explores the spiritual agonising of a religious man who sees his refusal to consent as a trial sent by God to test him. Those of you familiar with Kitano's other films will see in Takeshi's portrayal of this role a merging of the two distinct types that he usually plays. One is the Takeshi of *Sonatine*, which gives a similarly self-conscious portrait of fatigue at living in the modern world. The other is the Takeshi of *Hana-Bi*, and the sadness that stems simply from being human. Of course there are differences. The Takeshi of *Hana-Bi* is a remarkably decisive man. In *Settoku*, he gives a closely observed and very human portrait of the terrible strain of the decision he has to make. Mark Isham's music is the perfect foil to this drama about a religious crisis.

Unsurprisingly, before he started directing films himself, the film-makers who had been so lavish in their praise of *Okubo Kiyoshi no Hanzai* tried to get him to work with them. A notable example is Yojiro Takita's *Comic Magazine* (1986). Even though he only makes a brief appearance in the final scene, he steals the movie, again playing a role modelled on an actual crime. In the mid-eighties, although Japan was on course for an unprecedented economic boom, the warning signs of what was to come were already there. Shell companies with no capital backing appeared on the scene, defrauding pensioners of their savings. Takeshi plays a hit man with a social conscience who manages to get through the window of a small apartment where the boss of one such company has holed up to get away from the press, and kills him in a dramatic moment. Scenes from the actual murder were accidentally broadcast live on television, causing a sensation at the time. Although there is little facial or bodily resemblance between Takeshi and this man, the chillingly material quality is identical. This kind of cameo appearance is rare for

Okubo Kiyoshi no Hanzai

Takeshi, but by far and away the most memorable film was Takashi Ishii's more recent *Gonin* (1995) which employs a patchwork of radical techniques borrowed from Asian cinema. The macho gangster type he plays here is reminiscent of the Takeshi of *Boiling Point*.

Since becoming a director himself, the most noteworthy appearances he has made in a leading role are probably in Kazuo Kozumi's *Hoshi Wo Tsugumono* (Inheritors of Stars) (1990). Kitano himself came up with the original idea. And Toshihiro Tenma's *Many Happy Returns* (*Kyoso Tanjyo*) (1993) based on a story by Kitano himself. In both these, there are moments when Takeshi attains the status of a folk hero. In the former, Takeshi plays a sanka (these were traditional tribes of nomads who lived in the mountains of Japan before the state of Japan was created). In the latter he makes a double appearance, first as a member of a fraudulent modern religious sect, and then again right at the end as a tekiya, or racketeer (the tekiya are a breed of gypsy-like swindlers who pass off worthless rubbish to unsuspecting punters at traditional festivals, where they are an indispensable presence. They have their roots in the same tradition as the yakuza). These are good examples

of roles in which he has made use of his characteristic material quality outside the gangster type.

Of course it is the yakuza role that is the quintessential Takeshi. Apart from those already mentioned, other films worthy of note in this context are his first foray into Hollywood, Robert Longo's *Johnny Mnemonic* (1995); (this film, with its echoes of *Blade Runner* had some superb moments, but Takeshi's role was rather disappointing) and Jean-Pierre Limosin's *Tokyo Eyes* (1998).

But the Takeshi I would particularly like his overseas fans to know more about is the TV comedian, star of endless light entertainment shows, as there are scenes where you can see Takeshi, replete with material presence, actually moving along like a solid object in the manner of Buster Keaton. Sadly though, with the sole exception of a digest version called *Take-chan man henshin taiketsu-shu* (Takeshi-man's Transmogrification Showdown) featuring highlights from the enormously popular 1980's TV show *Oretachi Hyokinzoku* (The Band of Jokers), nothing has been released on video, even in Japan.

CANNES '99

"A heated 12 days in Cannes"

by Takako Imai

Takeshi Kitano's eighth film as a director, *Kikujiro*, was also his first to be shown in official competition at the Cannes Film Festival. His inclusion may have been taken for granted by critics but for Takeshi it was beyond his wildest dreams. A simple fact excited him – there he was, alongside such eminent directors as David Lynch, Leos Carax, Chen Kaige, Jim Jarmusch, Peter Greenaway and Pedro Almodovar, in the competition section of what is widely considered to be the most prestigious film festival in the world.

Kikujiro is a departure for Takeshi. The customary violence viewers have come to expect of his movies is nowhere to be seen. It's a heart warming road movie about a nine-year-old boy's search for the mother who abandoned him and the middle-aged slacker-type, played by Takeshi, who accompanies him on the quest. Well received at Cannes, there was soon talk that it could be a serious contender for an award, if not the Palme d'Or itself.

Tensions mounted but Takeshi remained enthusiastic and gave interviews to the international media. Two press conferences were organised exclusively for Japanese journalists. But the second one was cancelled at the last minute due to Takeshi's "fatigue" and he disappeared from public view.

Speculation turned to which award Takeshi would be taking home with him. The final day of the festival duly arrived on May 23 but the Japanese press contingent was confronted by an unexpected turn of events. Winners would usually expect to hear some kind of indication from the festival organisers by the afternoon, but staff of Nippon Herald, the Japanese distributor of *Kikujiro* were spotted away from the festival wearing casual clothes – not the formal evening wear obligatory at all official events.

So the awards ceremony rolled on. President of the jury David Cronenberg announced the winners

Takeshi on the balcony of the Palais des Festivals with producer Masayuki Mori

but neither the name Takeshi Kitano nor the title *Kikujiro* was mentioned. After the ceremony a spokesman for P2, Takeshi's publicists, made a statement to the deeply shocked Japanese press corps: "Thank you for your support. However, I would ask you to please leave Takeshi Kitano alone. Please don't try to follow and interview him."

Every journalist would abide with that request as they recalled Takeshi's sincerity when he said: "I was just happy to have been selected for nomination in this competition and I never even thought about winning." A heated 12 days in Cannes finally came to an end.

PRESS CONFERENCE

"I can't remember a time when my father wasn't drunk or violent," Takeshi says. "The whole family despised him. Of course he was my father, but we didn't have the kind of relationship you would normally have expected between a father and his children. So I described that kind of relationship in my script, using a situation in which a man can't help feeling awkward as he plays the role of a father to someone else's child. The reason why I named him Kikujiro was because I'm remembering my father by naming the character after him, instead of going to his graveside and giving my usual respects."

According to Takeshi, the story of Kikujiro developed as it was shot.

Takeshi surrounded by Japanese journalists

"Usually, I shoot in sequence from the start, but I only had a rough script in this case, so I went off in various directions," he explains. "Although I initially cast the kid in the main role, the story gradually focused more and more on the character of Kikujiro until finally it became a film about a man living for himself." Takeshi and producer Masayuki Mori insist they were not following the trend of recent films exploring the relationship between a child and an adult.

The question Takeshi found himself being asked most at Cannes was why had he stopped making violent films? "My films aren't violent films and I never made them only to show violence," he says, "Films are like food. You don't want to get tired of eating the same thing, so you try something different."

Yusuke Sekiguchi takes on the role of nine-year-old Masao in Kikujiro. Takeshi says it was Yusuke's lack of pretension that struck a chord with him. "I am not the manager of a circus and I didn't find him by touring around Japan," he adds. "We had about 200 kids gathered for the audition. Everybody came from drama schools and acting agencies so they looked very confident, and they seemed to be saying, 'Use me!' or, 'Don't I look cute?' However, there is always at least one child who lacks confidence and you wonder, 'Can he really be a child actor?' That's how I found Yusuke and I thought, 'He must have followed someone here by mistake'. There was something old fashioned about his appearance too. I thought that was a good thing, and if I could make audiences think he was cute, I would have achieved what I wanted."

Takeshi adopted a surprising approach in working with a child actor. "When directors use children, they usually look after them very well, but when I directed this film, I didn't think of him as a child," he says. "I thought of him as a dog rather than a human being. With a dog there would be no need for me to ever get angry. You can't teach animals how to act and kids never understand anyway. You

can only say things like: 'You better look down'. In the process of editing they look so sad with sad music and they look so happy with happy music. I think it is more unreasonable to request excessive acting from a child who can't think at all, rather than just treating him in the same way as a dog. The same principle applied when Yasujiro Ozu directed Chishu Ryu – he was like a Jizo effigy."

A sense of distance between the two lead actors is apparent in *Kikujiro*. Some Western viewers might find this difficult to appreciate but Takeshi points out that the Japanese, who for example shy away from kissing in public, have had to deal with a sense of distance in their lives. "What I wanted to emphasise was a sense of distance between the kid and Kikujiro. This is like traditional Japanese shyness. Although nowadays Japan is open to many Western cultures and it is now acceptable to express one's own feelings freely such as by crying or smiling, when I was small this sense of shyness, that I should try not to express my feelings, was drummed into me. I couldn't help making the film like this."

Joe Hisaishi, who has worked on a number of Takeshi's films including *A Scene At The Sea*, *Kids Return* and *Hana-Bi*, composed a striking score for

Kikujiro. This is an area where Takeshi also had an input for the first time. "In previous films I never discussed music with him. He just composed the music after I finished shooting. This time I asked him to compose the music beforehand. I talked with him about the music before filming, and at an early stage I handed him records I liked and made him listen to them. Among them there was a piece by George Winston and I thought it was rather nice imagining a scene where the kid is running, while I listened to it. Although Joe told me it was already perfect and he couldn't do the same kind of thing, the end result was very good. We were at our most adventurous when we intentionally put sad music in a comical scene, but I'm not sure whether this is successful or not."

Beat Kiyoshi from The Two Beats appears in a scene where Takeshi is waiting for a bus. Inevitably it turned comic. "When I shot that scene, Kiyoshi's stupid manager was standing beside the camera, laughing his head off," Takeshi recalls. "So I said, 'Hang on. We are making a film and not doing a stand-up in a music hall. Can't you do something with your laughter?' He then moved further away but was still laughing. The moment Kiyoshi sits besides me, it turned into a stand-up routine. I also laughed during the screening in Cannes. I thought there was no way but to turn that scene into stand-up comedy."

Takeshi was surprised some of the humour in the film worked so well with the Cannes audience. There were also scenes which he failed to realise would be regarded as humorous. "Some of the jokes went down a storm with a foreign audience. I thought only Japanese could understand them, especially as the subtitles break off in the middle because of the difficulty in translating the lines," he says. "I never expected that the alien played by Rakkyo Ide would be such a hit. I also found there was a difference in attitudes. It was pointed out to me that the military uniform which the costume

> **'Hang on. We are making a film and not doing a stand-up in a music hall. Can't you do something with your laughter?'**

designer chose was unintentionally like a Nazi's and that the map symbol of the Japanese temple resembles a swastika. I wasn't aware of these kind of things at all."

Some Western journalists went as far as questioning Takeshi's use of language in *Kikujiro*. "I was asked how common it was to use words like 'Stupid!' or 'Bastard!' In downtown Tokyo, people use 'Stupid!' as a cue for saying the following sentence, for example, 'Are you well, stupid?' or 'How are you, stupid? I was worried about you'. This doesn't imply they are angry but it's just a cue for the next line. Even when we go and see a patient at the hospital, we'd say, 'What's wrong with you, stupid?' or, 'Are you OK, stupid?' That's just typical downtown Tokyo speak."

A painting of an angel appears in *Kikujiro* just as one does in Takeshi's previous film *Hana-Bi*. Takeshi admits angels are really part of Western culture but like most people in Japan he treats them like a novelty because they are cute, without appreciating their religious significance.

"I used a different picture at first, but I didn't think it was suitable at all, so I used the angel painting instead out of desperation," he says.

Takeshi enjoys the creative freedom that making his own films gives him and strives to make movies with a 'timeless' feel. "At first, the basic rule in making films was to excite an audience by showing them 10 or so slides quickly, then when this inevitably became unsatisfactory, people started to add movement to pictures, and then this in turn became unsatisfactory, they added voices, and then music and then colour," he says. "Nowadays everybody is striving for technical progress by adding things, but eliminating things is another possibility. When I make films, I am always conscious about observing things from different angles. For example, I filmed a goldfish in a tank from above rather than doing it side-on in the

Nippon Herald's Japanese film poster for Kikujiro in Japan

water. I think some directors would go into the water and try to get as close as possible to the goldfish, whereas in my case, I sometimes look from above or sometimes from the side, trying to avoid going into water."

Takeshi admits his movies are "vague" in their settings. "I want to make timeless films, somewhere which is neither past nor present. It isn't good if I am conscious about the period," he says. *Kikujiro* was deliberately shot at locations where there were very few people around in order to avoid the location being identified. "I don't like to include features which symbolise a place such as Tokyo Tower. I intentionally chose to shoot in an unidentifiable place."

Takeshi wants to make a film in which a woman has a strong role, "because I have been often told I don't know how to portray women." But he doesn't entirely agree with that criticism. "Wasn't the girl in *A Scene At The Sea* nice even though she wasn't so beautiful? I like female characters who have that kind of charm. I know it is a bit of a departure from what everybody considers as beautiful, but I think it creates a good atmosphere for a movie." He has in mind a film about a suicide

Takeshi with Masayuki Mori in Cannes '99

pact, perhaps as a modern version of the *Chikamatsu-Shinjyu-Monogatari* tale.

Takeshi's talent and ability as a filmmaker were first recognised in Europe and at the Venice Film Festival in 1997 he picked up the Golden Lion for *Hana-Bi*. He is pleased *Kikujiro* is being shown in competition at Cannes but knows he should not take such things too seriously. "I was happy that I was being recognised in Europe while my films hadn't been successful in Japan. I thought if my films became popular overseas, they'd be like Hermès bags and Japanese people would soon be very keen on them. So I agreed to my films bring screened at the Venice Film Festival, as well as Cannes. Directors more highly acclaimed than me would probably say films should not be competing for prizes but at my level it is important that we go there.

"Japanese people think that everybody who makes films can go to Cannes – nonsense! When I

spoke to Nagisa Oshima the other day, he said: 'It took 10 years for me to get to participate in the competition at Cannes. I think it will also take you just as long'. It's like climbing a ladder. So I'm already honoured with being in the competition and I don't expect anything beyond that. In Venice it was pure luck that I was able to win, and I don't expect to be so lucky a second time."

But there are huge expectations surrounding his next project, a film called *Brother*, which is being produced by Jeremy Thomas, who made *Merry Christmas, Mr. Lawrence*. It will be Takeshi's first film in English. "We've started preparations but we haven't completed a script or decided how to deal with the English language yet," he reveals. "If someone goes to America for the first time, they wouldn't be able to speak a word of English, and while that is one possibility for the setting, I still don't know yet exactly what is going to happen."

MILLENNIUM FILM: BROTHER

Takeshi Kitano is teaming up again with producer Jeremy Thomas for his next movie *Brother*. With a budget of £10 million, *Brother* is a collaboration between Jeremy's Recorded Picture Company and Kitano's own production company, Office Kitano. It will be shot, predominantly in English, on location in Los Angeles and Tokyo. Filming gets under way in November 1999, with a release date scheduled for late 2000.

"I met Takeshi and Masayuki Mori at a dinner we gave at the London Film Festival three or four years ago, when I was chairman of the British Film Institute," says Jeremy. "We were reminiscing about old times, and I said to him, 'I'd love to make a movie with you again. I'd love to work with you as a producer if you want to do something. They were saying they were thinking about making a film in America and that was the start."

Based on an original screenplay by Takeshi, *Brother* is the story of a Yakuza type and his journey from Tokyo to downtown LA and beyond. "It's completely different from other films he's made but there is a link," says Jeremy, who is hoping *Brother* will also appeal to mainstream Western audiences. "We'll try to do what we did with *Merry Christmas, Mr. Lawrence*, which is still a very popular film."

ACKNOWLEDGEMENTS

Bibliography

Asakusa Kid by Beat Takeshi published by Shincho-sha

Takeshi-kun Hai! by Beat Takeshi published by Shincho-sha

Takeshi No Shinutameno Ikikata by Beat Takeshi published by Shincho-sha

Ganmen Mahi by Beat Takeshi published by Ota Shuppan

Watashiwa Sekaide Kirawareru by Beat Takeshi published by Shincho-sha

Geijyutsu Shincho January 1996 - May 1997 issue in the Takeshi No Benjyo No Rakugaki section published by Shincho-sha

Shincho 45 special issue "Comaneci!" published by Shincho-sha

Photo Credits

Cover Photo: by Greg Gorman © Office Kitano Inc. Inside Front Cover & Inside Back Cover (from *Sonatine*): Bandai p.4 copyright Andrea Merola; pp5, 6, 7, 8 courtesy ICA; pp14-15 Sankei Shimbun-sha; p.16-25 courtesy ICA; p.26 Bandai (top), Celluloid Dreams (bottom); pp27-29 Bandai; p.30 Celluloid Dreams (top), Nippon Herald (bottom); p.31 P2; p.32 courtesy ICA; pp33-35 Bandai; p.36 Alliance Releasing (top), Bandai (bottom left & right); p.37 Nippon Herald; p.38 courtesy Office Kitano Inc. (top), Nippon Herald (bottom); pp39-41 courtesy Office Kitano Inc.; p.42 courtesy Recorded Picture Company; pp43-52, 54-56, 59-64 copyright Recorded Picture Company; p.68 Sankei Shimbun-sha; p.72 courtesy Office Kitano; p.73 courtesy ICA (left), courtesy Office Kitano (right); pp74-78 courtesy ICA; p.80 Bandai; p.81 Bandai (top), ICA (bottom); p.82 copyright Andrea Merola; p.83 courtesy Alliance Releasing; p.84 P2; pp85-86 courtesy Alliance Releasing; p. 87 courtesy Alliance Releasing (top), copyright Andrea Merola (bottom); pp88-89 copyright Andrea Merola; p.90 courtesy ICA (top), courtesy Alliance Releasing (bottom); p.91 copyright Andrea Merola; p.92 © Office Kitano Inc.; p.93 RM Europe; pp94-103 © Office Kitano Inc.; pp104-106 courtesy Yumi Shirakawa; p.107 Sankei Shimbun-sha; p.110 copyright Recorded Picture Company; p.111-112 courtesy ICA p.114 TBS; p.115 copyright Recorded Picture Company; pp116, 117, 119 TBS p.120 copyright Jean-Louis Tornato; p.121 courtesy Nippon Herald (top), copyright Jean-Louis Tornato (bottom); p.122 courtesy Office Kitano Inc. (top), copyright Jean-Louis Tornato (bottom); p.123 courtesy Office Kitano Inc.; p.125 courtesy Nippon Herald; p.126 copyright Kazuko Wakayama (top), courtesy Office Kitano Inc. (bottom); p.127 courtesy Office Kitano Inc.

RM EUROPE

Japanese/English Interpretation and Translation Courses

If you are interested in training to become an interpreter or translator in the Japanese and English languages please contact us by telephone or email for details of our courses.

We are also looking for good interpreters, translators, assistant teachers, writers, editors, and book projects.
Please contact us or send details to,

RM EUROPE
24 Broomgrove Gardens, Edgware, Middx. HA8 5J UK
Tel: 020 8952 5302 Email: sales@rmeurope.co.uk website: www.rmeurope.co.uk